SECRET CLEVELAND

A GUIDE TO THE WEIRD,
WONDERFUL, AND OBSCURE

D1557411

Deb Thompson & Tonya Prater

Library of Congress Control Number: 2017934678

ISBN: 9781681061085

Design by Jill Halpin

Printed in the United States of America
17 18 19 20 21 5 4 3 2 1

To all the wanderers and travelers who seek to find the weird, wonderful and obscure in every place you visit. May your quest for the unique and bizarre never be quenched.

CONTENTS

INTRODUCTION

Some of our favorite road trip memories stem from finding the most off-the-beaten-path attractions. Searching out weird and sometimes senseless facts and trivia about a destination has led us on epic journeys that we never knew existed. Taking that journey through Cleveland has been a whirlwind of fun discoveries and surprises.

The more we explored, the more we uncovered. Just when we thought we knew the answers, we discovered something else. Literary research turned into finding a "door" to another universe and tiny patrons. Searching for Lake Erie creatures led to finding a wall of whales and hidden salt mines. A quest for finding more about past presidents had us staring down a weeping angel and visiting a church that held memorial services for two assassinated American presidents. Lacing up our hiking boots to find the best paths turned into a trek to a bridge that led to nowhere, picturesque waterfalls, and a house straight out of the dinosaur age. Scouting for unique and interesting museums led us to saints and a savior. Looking for more adventurous oddities led us to every adrenaline junkie's dream and a ride that goes through the roof. Every weird, wonderful, and obscure corner we turned led to another fantastic discovery.

Unearthing these places in Cleveland, an artsy and cultural destination full of experiences and as diverse as the people who call the city home, has been a fact-finding mission that would make Sherlock Holmes proud. We have only scratched the surface of what Cleveland has to offer. We know there are many more interesting stories lurking in the shadows if you just take the time to look. Use this book as a guide to jumpstart your own secret adventures in and around the city that gave Americans some of their greatest treasures: rock and roll, Superman, and *A Christmas Story*.

\underline{1} A CHRISTMAS STORY HOUSE

Do you have a Red Ryder?

"I want an official Red Ryder, carbine action, two-hundred-shot range model air rifle!"
    "No, you'll shoot your eye out."

Famous words from an American cult classic movie that are quoted or heard, at some point, by almost everyone. Walking through the yard where Ralphie shot his coveted Red Ryder can only happen at *A Christmas Story House* in the Tremont West neighborhood of Cleveland.

Ralphie's house really does exist, and, luckily for movie lovers everywhere, it is open to the public for tours. Visit the kitchen invaded by turkey grubbing dogs, walk the staircase that Ralphie walked down in his pink bunny suit, see the living room where Christmas was unwrapped, and ultimately play in the yard where Ralphie shot his Red Ryder. Although the inside of the house isn't the actual set used in the movie, the outside of the house and the yard is the exact location where the movie was filmed.

Scenes from the inside of the house were shot on a set in Los Angeles, but as luck would have it, an *A Christmas Story* aficionado purchased the home in 2004 and recreated the interior to be an exact replica of the movie. A quarter of a million dollars and two years later the home opened for others to enjoy.

The only place in the world where you can play in Ralphie's yard and walk through *A Christmas Story* house.

In a quiet neighborhood, near city center, you can step into the set of one of America's favorite cult classic movies, A Christmas Story. Walk in Ralphie's footsteps as you wander through the house and play in the yard. © Deb Thompson

A CHRISTMAS STORY HOUSE

WHAT Movie location

WHERE 3159 W. 11th St.

COST $11

PRO TIP A Christmas Story House is now offering overnight stays! Contact them to book your stay.

Today, a museum and gift shop neighbor the house to create an entire *A Christmas Story* movie campus, with numerous photo opportunities.

Extra points to those who take selfies in a pink bunny costume in front of the house.

2 A CITY FARM

Who says you can't have a pig in the city?

In the center of downtown, amid crazy traffic, rushing people, and endless activity, there is a small urban farm. Located against a wall of the Huntington Convention Center, you'll find bees buzzing about, collecting pollen to make sweet honey, chickens pecking the ground and laying eggs, and, just because, a lazy hog or two sunning themselves while relaxing in the dirt.

Having an urban farm isn't a new concept, but having one that is owned and operated by a restaurant in the middle of the city is new for Cleveland. The farm is all thanks to Matt Del Regno, executive chef for Levy Restaurants. He started planting the seeds of increasing awareness for responsible food sourcing to the powers that be, and the idea grew. When the idea was ripe for picking, the farm was started.

First came the bees, then the chickens and pigs, and finally the herb and vegetable plots. When this endeavor began, there were just a few hives. Now twelve hives house more than 60,000 bees that produce 1,000 pounds of honey per year. The honey, as well as the eggs from the chickens, are used by Levy Restaurants at the Convention Center. The pigs, a reminder to only serve Ohio pork, are used for breeding purposes only.

This urban farm is proof that sustainable farm-to-table foods can happen next to high-rises and highways.

AN URBAN FARM IN THE MIDDLE OF THE CITY

WHAT Farm

WHERE 300 Lakeside Ave. E

COST Free

PRO TIP The overlook at the Convention Center provides a view to the farm below.

Using a small tract of land between the Convention Center and railroad tracks, a farm has been installed as a new home for chickens, pigs, and bees. The eggs and honey are used by the Convention Center catering group.

Down on the farm in the middle of the city at the Huntington Convention Center, where bees, chickens, and pigs roam.

3 A RIVER RUNS THROUGH IT

How many bridges span the Cuyahoga River?

The river twists and turns through the city, flowing closer and closer to its final destination. It has had an arduous eighty-five-mile journey that ends at Lake Erie. For years, the river was polluted with dark inky waters. Fortunately, it has been cleaned up and sparkles brightly, making it the perfect backdrop for the numerous photogenic bridges that cross it.

Today, a number of bridges are open and used for automotive traffic. To find the best Instagrammable bridges, head downtown and off the highway.

The massive, arched Veterans Memorial Bridge has starred in a number of Hollywood films. The Veterans Memorial Bridge has a lower level that is closed to traffic but is occasionally open for public walking tours.

The Center Street Swing Bridge has a base on each shore that swings the bridge away from the water so that large vessels can pass. It's much like a drawbridge except instead of moving the bridge into a vertical position, the bridge remains horizontal and is swung toward land. It is quite the site to watch this bridge in operation.

The Main Avenue Bridge is a cantilever truss bridge and is one of Ohio's longest elevated structures, stretching out

A RIVER RUNS THROUGH IT

WHAT Bridges

WHERE Various locations

COST Free

PRO TIP Park at the nearby Westside Market and walk to the Hope Memorial Bridge. A pedestrian lane is available.

© *Library of Congress: Vertical bridges, swing bridges, arch bridges, and more all cross the Cuyahoga River, providing a variety of photo opportunities and a prime spot for bridge enthusiasts to visit. http://www.loc.gov/pictures/resource/hhh.oh0124.photos.125722p/*

8,000 feet. The Willow Avenue Bridge is a vertical lift bridge that leads to Whiskey Island. Its unique construction allows the entire bridge to be lifted straight up and out of the way of passing ship traffic.

Those are all lovely to see, but it is probably safe to say that the Hope Memorial Bridge is the most photographed for its four, 43-foot-tall Guardians of Transportation, each holding a different type of vehicle, that stand sentinel over passing traffic.

Be sure to charge up your camera battery because these unique bridges, sprinkled throughout Cleveland, are a must stop and photo worthy.

<u>4</u> A WALK IN THE WOODS

Could this possibly be the largest arboretum in the United States?

Exit the highway and start the drive down a paved yet hilly road where the speed limit slows you down to a mere thirty-five mph. The slower pace allows you to enjoy all the rolling hills that are visible from your car window. Five miles after exiting the highway, you'll arrive at Holden Arboretum, said to be one of the largest arboretums in the United States.

You are now surrounded by thousands of acres of land, 3,400 to be exact, that is all about trees. This is the home to 9,400 different kinds of woody plants from 79 different plant families. It's about as diverse as an arboretum can be given its cooler midwestern climate.

In addition to trees, guests are treated to a variety of flower gardens: a butterfly garden, Ohio wildflower garden, and a display garden are all within an easy walk of the parking area. The display garden showcases what is currently in bloom throughout the arboretum and the region.

Because of the vast range of ecosystems alive in Holden, the land has been organized into fourteen natural areas. Six of the natural areas are available as part of the twenty miles

---

Take a walk in one of the largest arboretums in the United States, with 3,400 acres of land and 9,400 varieties of woody plants plus two National Natural Landmarks.

One of the largest arboretums located within the United States, Holden Arboretum in Lake County offers a diverse selection of plants and trees that are easily accessible from the many groomed walking trails.

A WALK IN THE WOODS

WHAT Arboretum

WHERE 9550 Sperry Rd., Kirtland

COST $10

PRO TIP For a look from above, be sure to climb above the trees at the Emergent Tower.

of trail systems, while the remaining eight are only available on a limited basis and only as part of a guided hike.

Two of the natural areas have been designated as National Natural Landmarks: the public Bole Woods and the North Stebbins Gulch. To date, there are only about 600 natural areas with a National Natural Landmark designation.

5 ABANDONED SUBWAY

What happened to the Detroit-Superior Subway?

Deep beneath the city streets of Cleveland, there once was a small subway system that took streetcars from light to dark and back as it transported commuters. Moving from West 25th and Detroit to West 9th, riders only caught glimpses of light as they crossed on the lower level of the Detroit-Superior Bridge. Sadly, the system lasted only a few years before economic hardship shut it down.

In an attempt to utilize part of the subway system for modern transportation, the tracks were ripped from the lower level of the bridge and pavement was laid for use as an automotive crossing. After too many cars hit the support structures, the city quickly shut down the lower lanes, and the entrances to both the lower part of the bridge and the subway were sealed off to the public.

Shuttered for more than 50 years, what remains beneath is a mystery that is seldom seen by the public. Occasionally, the Department of Public Works will open the tunnels and the lower level of the bridge for tours, but mostly this dark underworld remains unseen. Remnants of a streetcar,

ABANDONED SUBWAY

WHAT Detroit-Superior Bridge and Subway

WHERE Detroit Ave.

COST Free

PRO TIP Great views of the bridge can be had from Heritage Park.

© *Library of Congress: The architecture of the subway remains hidden away in the underbelly of the Detroit-Superior Subway system. It sits empty today, seldom seen by residents or visitors alike. http://www.loc.gov/pictures/item/oh0124.photos.125731p/*

tracks leading to nowhere, and elaborate stonework is hidden beneath the heart of the city, with no plan to revitalize and expand this mode of public transportation.

More than 50 years ago, Clevelanders used the Detroit-Superior Subway for transportation under the busy street above.

<u>6</u> ALL THAT JAZZ

Which first lady commissioned bowls from Cowan Pottery?

Here's a hint. It is 1930, and potter Guy Cowan has been back from the war, the First World War, that is, for about a decade. Prior to serving his country, he made a living by throwing clay. Upon returning from war he moved his studio to Rocky River and started to build a successful commercial business.

To help make that happen he hired a staff of skilled artisans. Artists Elizabeth Anderson, Thelma Frazier Winter, and Viktor Schreckengos filled his employee database. Due to all the creative skill that was now part of Cowan Pottery, the company was incredibly successful and the pottery was sold around the country.

One day a request arrived for a New York City–inspired punch bowl. Viktor Schreckengos filled the order by creating a unique bowl with a bold "jazz" design and a blue glaze that reminded him of New York City at night. Shipping it off for approval, he promptly received a request for two more and discovered that the bowls had been commissioned by none other than Eleanor Roosevelt. After fulfilling the first lady's request for the additional Jazz Bowls, the design was put into production. Sadly, only a handful of bowls were produced due to the Great Depression, which caused Cowan Pottery to fail in 1931.

All is not lost, though. Today, over 1,300 pieces of Cowan Pottery are on display at the Cowan Pottery Museum located in the Rocky River Public Library, about fifteen minutes from Cleveland. The museum includes both prewar and postwar pieces and, most important, you can view one of the famous Jazz Bowls.

A New York City pattern adorns a punchbowl designed for First Lady Eleanor Roosevelt by Cowen Pottery is showcased at the Cowen Pottery Museum inside the Rocky River Public Library. © Deb Thompson

ALL THAT JAZZ

WHAT Museum

WHERE 1600 Hampton Rd., Rocky River

COST Free

PRO TIP A Jazz Bowl is also on display at the Cleveland Museum of Art.

Cowan Pottery, including the famous Jazz Bowls, were thrown and fired in a Cleveland suburb. These are now on display in the Cowan Pottery Museum.

7 AN ARCHITECTURAL MARVEL

What is eating that building?

It appears as if molten silver were slowly engulfing a building as the undulating metal rises out of the ground and begins to surround the red brick. The curves and lines of this structure feel a bit out of place in this otherwise sedate University area, but that makes the Peter B. Lewis Building stand out that much more.

This is home to the Weatherhead School of Business on the campus of Case Western Reserve University, but the real lesson here is how the world-renowned architect Frank Gehry uses metal, brick, and wide open spaces to create a spectacular architectural design both inside and out. The roof resembles that of ocean waves, but curiously enough, the interior ceiling matches this same flow of movement. Unbeknownst to many who enter these hallowed halls, the east side of the building is four stories, whereas the west side is five stories, and, surprisingly, the two sides do not connect, causing confusion for first-time students and visitors.

It has been more than fifteen years since the building was completed, and it still stands strong. It's proof that school buildings can be just as intriguing and interesting on the outside as learning is on the inside.

A unique architectural structure stands apart from the other sedate buildings on the campus of Case Western Reserve University.

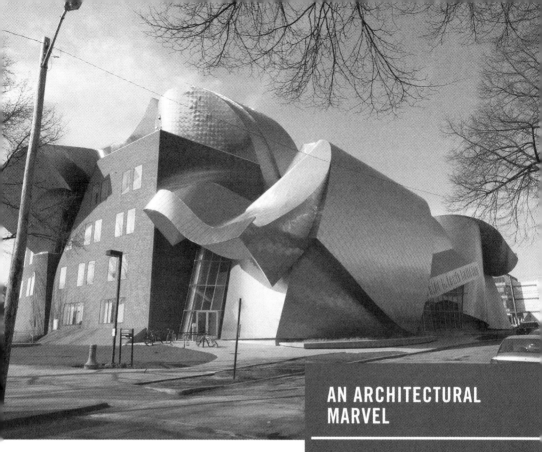

AN ARCHITECTURAL MARVEL

A visit to a big city isn't required in order to enjoy Frank Gehry architecture. Simply head to the campus of Western Case Reserve and see how Gehry incorporates flowing metal and brick into one amazing building. © Deb Thompson

WHAT Peter B. Lewis Building

WHERE 11119 Bellflower Rd.

COST Free

PRO TIP Street parking available

8 AUT-O-RAMA DRIVE-IN THEATER

What could be better than going to the cinema?

For many drive-ins around the country, the lights have faded, the gates have closed, and the silver screen has lit up for the last time. Drive-ins have become a novelty of the past. Something from a bygone era, drive-ins have been pushed aside and lost thanks to the advancement and technology of digital movies.

Still, what teenagers (and some adults) don't have memories of stealing a few kisses, or more, in the back of a car parked at the drive-in? Or crowding a dozen friends in the vehicle for carload night? And don't get me started on the triple feature, which makes for a heck of a long movie-watching evening.

Though these attractions are becoming few and far between, you'll find the Aut-O-Rama Drive-in in North Ridgeville has been in operation and thriving since 1965. Family owned and operated, the Aut-O-Rama was the first drive-in in the area to feature movies on two screens and is a must while in the Cleveland area.

Don't miss the opportunity to watch blockbuster movies under the stars on a warm summer night at a drive-in theater.

This drive-in theater is a treat for movie goers during the warmer spring and summer months. Pack up the family and enjoy a movie under the stars. ©Tonya Prater

AUT-O-RAMA DRIVE-IN

WHAT Drive-in

WHERE 33395 Lorain Rd., North Ridgeville

COST $10

PRO TIP Arrive early to ensure you find the perfect parking spot for the best views.

Today you can enjoy the warm summer nights as you relax in a lounge chair and munch on popcorn from the onsite concession stand that sells all your favorite movie fixin's, and a few that aren't as common, like cotton candy, while you listen to the movie in Dolby FM stereo sound. You'll find movie offerings ranging from the classics of yesteryear to today's blockbuster hits.

So, next time you want to escape the house and watch a movie but don't want to get dressed, consider a trip to the drive-in, which like your local Walmart (or big box store) will welcome you even in your PJs.

$\underline{9}$ BAYarts

Can you find the Thriving Arts Community near the Shores of Lake Erie?

BAYarts is a secret gem in Bay Village. Tucked into the trees of the Cleveland Metroparks on the Huntington Reservation and across the road from Huntington Beach (which offers one of the best views of Cleveland from the shore), this campus of historic buildings is easily overlooked by those passing through Cleveland.

Founded in 1948, the BAYarts campus was established by artists who hoped to share their love of art with the community through classes and other events. In 2005, a group of volunteers spearheaded a campaign to revitalize the grounds and now has become a resource for local

families that offer classes, events, and summer camps. But for those passing through the area, you'll find the home of John Huntington, a wealthy Cleveland industrialist, the Victorian-style Irene Fuller Home that serves as a classroom and gallery and was also the site where infamous Sam Sheppard was arrested for the murder of his wife in the 1950's, a station house and historic caboose.

A shop on the campus features items from both professional and up-and-coming artists in two galleries that contain an eclectic collection of items that range from upcycled projects to clothing, to books, to items that celebrate Cleveland.

This historic community is easy to miss if you don't know it's there, but to the community of Bay Village, it offers a thriving art scene that is open to visitors. ©Tonya Prater

BAYarts

WHAT BAYarts

WHERE Huntington Reservation in Cleveland Metroparks

COST Free to visit

PRO TIP Clear your schedule and roam the campus of BAYarts before wandering across the street to Huntington Beach for a picnic.

Visiting adults may enjoy a glass of wine at Vento, the wine bar, while kids will be enamored with the on-site caboose and nearby Lake Erie Nature & Science Center.

BAYarts offers a unique setting for artists in the Cleveland Metroparks and has a surprising connection to one of Cleveland's most infamous murders.

<u>10</u> BELLY UP TO THE BAR

Who was shot here?

Quench your thirst with an ice-cold lager and prepare yourself for a great story when you visit the Great Lakes Brewing Company. Amble on over to the bar, pull up a stool, ask the barkeep to pull you a draft of Eliot Ness Amber Lager, and then casually ask about the bullet holes in the wall.

The company took three Victorian-era buildings and merged them. One building was the Elton, a former hotel and burlesque house, another was the McClean's Feed & Seed Company, and the third was the Market Tavern, a popular watering hole back in the day. Of course, being a popular watering hole meant that Elliot Ness spent a fair amount of time here enjoying a pint or two. Each of the three buildings has a pretty interesting history but none as good as the story that surrounds the bullet holes.

Elliot Ness was a famous American Prohibition agent in the late 1920s. He was the leader of a group of men called The Untouchables. The group of agents worked diligently to bring down gangster Al Capone in Chicago in the early 1930s. Afterward, around 1935, Ness moved to Cleveland and worked on cleaning up the streets. Here he brought down two hundred crooked police officers and fifteen other public officials.

The bullet holes can be seen in the woodwork behind the bar in the former Market Tavern building. The story goes that the bullet holes in the walls came from the gun of Elliot Ness or were bullets aimed at Mr. Ness that missed. History is unclear as to why he may have discharged his gun or why a gun may have been fired at him, but regardless, the story is a good one to enjoy while enjoying a pint at the same bar Mr. Ness once frequented.

The Great Lakes Brewing Company is keeping history alive behind its bar. Bullet holes, said to be from Elliot Ness's gun or perhaps from a gun aimed at him, remain to this day, almost one hundred years later. © Deb Thompson

BELLY UP TO THE BAR

WHAT Brewery

WHERE 2516 Market Ave.

COST Free to see bullet holes

PRO TIP Elliot Ness is buried in Lakeside Cemetery.

Belly up to the bar and enjoy a pint while listening to stories of days gone by and how those bullet holes behind the bar came to be.

11 BESSIE: LAKE ERIE'S SEA SERPENT

Have you seen the Lake Erie Monster?

It's the early 1800s and the sloop *Felicity* is sailing across Lake Erie, full of weather-hardened seamen who are hard at work. Suddenly, something surfaces in the water and catches the eye of one of the mariners, who then calls out to his mates. The crew gathers together as a thirty- to forty-foot-long creature swims through the water. Unable to identify it, the men return to shore and share their story with all who will listen.

Fast forward a couple hundred years and there are still sightings of this brownish, snakelike creature. Some speculate that the monster, known as Bessie or South Shore Bessie, is simply a very large sturgeon, a Lake Erie fish that is said to live up to 150 years and can be up to seven feet long and weigh 300 pounds. Sturgeon do look prehistoric and are bottom feeders, seldom coming to the surface, which could explain the intermittent Lake Erie Monster sightings.

© Library of Congress: A freighter leaves the Cuyahoga River and heads out onto Lake Erie to transport goods and hopes to not bump into the infamous Lake Erie Monster, Bessie. http://www.loc.gov/pictures/item/det1994020597/PP/

At one time Huron Lagoons Marina was offering a $100,000 reward for the unharmed and safe capture of the Lake Erie Monster. If you happen to be cruising the lake and are able to capture Bessie, it may be worth a call to see if the reward is still available. To date, it has not been claimed.

Do you believe a sea monster lives in the water of Lake Erie? Reports say it has been spotted many times over the years but has never been captured.

12 BIG FUN TOY STORE

Do you know where to find the coolest toy store on earth?

Do you have a collection of toys from your childhood taking up space in your attic? Now may be the time to gather your vintage collection and head to Cleveland Heights to the Big Fun Toy Store to swap out some of your old stuff for new-to-you stuff, or sell your toys and put some cold hard cash in your pocket. Big Fun is unlike any toy store in the area. Heralded by locals as the Greatest Toy Store on Earth, this toy store is better than any you've ever entered before.

An interesting blend of pure geekiness and a blast from the past, stepping inside the door is like stepping into a rich relative's play room that has been hidden away for years. You'll find one-of-a-kind toys and collectibles from the '50s, '60s, and '70s on the stocked-to-capacity shelves mixed with Cleveland souvenirs, classic candy, and fun and quirky novelties like Unicorn Bandages and Grow Your Own Weed, um, for medicinal purposes, right? Okay, maybe it's fake, but it's a fun thought for someone on your shopping list.

The Cleveland Heights store has helped gift buyers select the perfect gift for birthdays, Christmas, or just because for over twenty-five years and is worth the stop whether you're a serious buyer or simply browsing. You never know what you may find inside the Big Fun Toy Store!

The Big Fun Toy Store is not just for kids. This is one stop that mom and pop and even grandma and grandpa will enjoy.

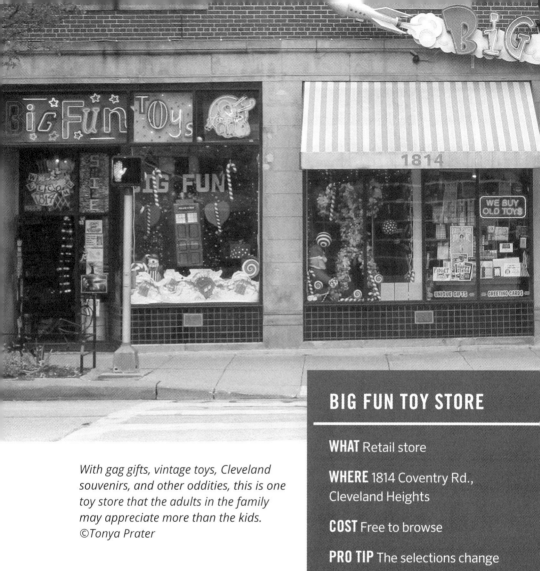

With gag gifts, vintage toys, Cleveland souvenirs, and other oddities, this is one toy store that the adults in the family may appreciate more than the kids.
©*Tonya Prater*

BIG FUN TOY STORE

WHAT Retail store

WHERE 1814 Coventry Rd., Cleveland Heights

COST Free to browse

PRO TIP The selections change daily, so stop back often.

13 BRIDGE TO NOWHERE

Where does the bridge go?

Take the brick-lined street that curves up the side of a hill to Hillandale Park. Shortly after reaching the top, the road will end and the forest stretches out across hills and ravines. Something is hiding amongst the trees that will be quite surprising to most visitors. A short way down the path hikers will stumble upon a most unusual site, an elaborate concrete vehicle bridge with nine supporting arches and guard rails that connect one hill to the other and spans a shallow ravine.

This unassuming "Bridge to Nowhere" sits just off Hillandale Park in Euclid. It was built in the 1920s for a proposed subdivision. Unfortunately, the project tanked when the Great Depression of 1929 hit and destroyed the economy. The bridge was left unattended, no subdivision to be built, and the bridge was quickly forgotten.

Today, the bridge is slowly crumbling and being taken over by nature as it is methodically being covered by grass, leaves, and weeds. The bridge is open to walk across, but years of decay has left holes in the road, and the loss of guard rails creates a cross at your own risk situation. In the ravine below, where the bridge legs appear to stand

---

In the middle of the forest behind a quiet subdivision sits a bridge that time has forgotten and which leads to nowhere.

This multi-arched bridge was built to transport cars across a shallow ravine for a proposed subdivision. Sadly, the subdivision fell on economic hard times, but the bridge remains for hikers to enjoy. © Deb Thompson

BRIDGE TO NOWHERE

WHAT Bridge

WHERE 27598 Tremaine Dr., Hillandale Park, Euclid

COST Free

PRO TIP Park at the end of the road and follow short trail to bridge. Wear good hiking shoes, as it's a hilly area.

strong, graffiti artists and partiers have spray-painted the concrete supports, providing a visual explosion of colors on an otherwise drab structure.

Sadly, the bridge was never used for its intended purpose. It was abandoned by the owners and now sits as a reminder of what might have been, with no plan or purpose for its future.

14 CLEVELAND GRAYS ARMORY MUSEUM

How will a city protect itself without a police force?

Built on what was once the edge of the city, Gray's Armory was constructed to house Cleveland's first military organization. The city militia was formed after a rash of seven burglaries swept through the city in one year, and the wealthy feared a metropolis overtaken by crime would result if not swiftly dealt with. Because there was no police force at the time, a militia was formed in 1837 to protect the streets of Cleveland.

The Grays took their role of protector seriously and, during the Civil War, when asked by President Lincoln to support the nation in combat, they answered the battle cry. They were the first regiment on the battlefield at Manassas (or Bull Run) and continued to support the United States in battle until after World War I, when independent militias were disbanded.

The home of the Cleveland Grays Armory was built in 1893. Built prior to Severance Hall or the I-X Center, this historic property was the location of Cleveland's first concert season for the Cleveland Orchestra, the first performance of the Cleveland Opera, and the site of the first auto show in Cleveland.

Today you may tour the museum to learn the history of what was the precursor of the National Guard, visit the firing range in the basement of the Armory, or attend a lecture, educational function, or private social event in America's oldest independently owned Armory.

The militia may no longer exist, but the Grays continue to serve the community of Cleveland to this day by ensuring their history is never forgotten.

CLEVELAND GRAYS ARMORY MUSEUM

WHAT Museum

WHERE 1234 Bolivar Rd.

COST Free

PRO TIP Free public tours are offered the first Wednesday of the month from 12 p.m. to 4 p.m.

Home of Grays Armory, a precursor of the police force, this eye-catching building with unique architectural elements was built in the late 1800s and has served an important role in Cleveland's history. © Deb Thompson

A rash of seven burglaries in one year left the citizens of Cleveland scurrying for protection. The result was a city-wide militia.

15 CLEVELAND POLICE MUSEUM

What were the Torso Murders, and why were they significant?

Do you find yourself binge watching reruns of *CSI*, *Law & Order*, and *Criminal Minds*? If you answered yes, the Cleveland Police Museum, located in the Justice Center, is for you. Opened in 1983, the museum documents over one hundred years of Cleveland police force history with information and artifacts dating back to 1866. With over 4,000 square feet of exhibits, this museum remains one of the only law enforcement museums of its kind open to the public within the United States.

The museum houses the original Murphy Call Box that was invented in 1890 and that allowed police officers working in the neighborhoods to communicate with the precinct. You'll learn about Eliot Ness, hired by the mayor to be Cleveland's Safety Director at a time when the city was voted one of the top five most dangerous cities in the country. Ness worked tirelessly to combat crime, and by the time he left the force he had succeeded in nearly eliminating crime and corruption on the streets of Cleveland. Yet the resolution of one crime spree eluded him. He was never

CLEVELAND POLICE MUSEUM

WHAT Museum

WHERE 1300 Ontario St.

COST Free

PRO TIP You must go through security to enter the museum, so leave your valuables and pocket knives in your vehicle.

The museum is housed inside the Cleveland Police Headquarters Building in the Justice Center. Visit this museum to learn the history of the police force and see some most unusual artifacts from past crimes. © Deb Thompson

able to crack the Kingsbury Run murders, though it is speculated that he knew who was behind the gruesome Torso Murders; he simply lacked evidence to convict.

The Torso Murders are considered the work of one of America's first serial killers. The murderer targeted the indigent and those who worked and lived in a shady area of the city. Of the thirteen dismembered victims, only three were identified. In hopes of identifying the victims, four death masks were made, some using the victim's own hair, and displayed at the World's Fair in Cleveland in 1936. The death masks are now on display in the Cleveland Police Museum.

Before leaving the museum, make sure to get a selfie inside the jail cell.

Crime buffs will love this museum with exhibits that range from a robot that retrieves bombs to creepy artifacts of one of the nation's most well-known unsolved murders.

16 CLEVELAND PUBLIC LIBRARY

What does the largest library collection of chess sets, miniature books and a Great Wall of China brick all have in common?

There are so much more than books within the walls of the Cleveland Public Library. Wander around this 1925 building, pass through doors, wander under arched, tiled ceilings, and climb grand marble staircases. Soon, you'll discover an entire world beyond the typical books and you enter a place of art, collections and culture.

The marble building itself is a work of art with historic ceilings, antique light fixtures, decorative metal works, and leather doors. It's the third-floor Special Collections department that is the real charmer though. The area is filled with interesting treasures that have been acquired over many years. The department is most famous for housing the world's largest library collection of chess sets and chess materials. There is so much more beyond that though. A collection of miniature books, at one time the

---

The Cleveland Public Library is so much more than a place to check out books. It is part library, part museum and all inspiration. A great place to wile away an afternoon or a rainy day.

The special collections department at the Cleveland Public Library is home to one of the largest collections of chess sets in the world and an incredible collection of miniature books. © Deb Thompson

CLEVELAND PUBLIC LIBRARY

WHAT Art

WHERE 325 Superior Ave.

COST Free

PRO TIP On the third-floor exhibition corridor be sure to look closely at the wrought iron display cases for small iron owls strategically placed to hold up the cases.

largest in the world, includes some books so small a magnifying glass is required to read them. There are historic playbills from over one hundred years of performances at the Cleveland Play House. A brick from the Great Wall of China in on display as well as folklore items, architectural drawings and so much more.

All art and artifacts are relegated to the third floor. There are permanent art displays and exhibits throughout the building making this a real cultural gem for Cleveland.

17 CLEVELAND TOURS

Why explore Cleveland on your own when you can join a tour?

If you want to get the most out of your time in Cleveland and don't want to spend all day circling downtown in your vehicle looking for a parking spot, consider one of the many tours that are offered in the city.

Segway Tours—Save your feet some steps and glide around Cleveland on a Segway. It only takes a few minutes of practice to get used to operating the Segway before you'll feel like a pro. Then hit the streets with confidence. Ninety-minute tours of downtown are available and take you to some lesser-known areas of Cleveland.

Walking Tours—Lace up your walking shoes and hit the pavement with Take a Hike walking tours. You'll learn the history of Cleveland through ninety-minute tours that feature actors and actresses portraying historical figures from Cleveland's past on your route. Five tours are available that cover the Gateway District, Warehouse District, Playhouse Square, Canal Basin Park in the Flats, and the Civic Center.

Lolly the Trolley Tours—Enjoy a climate-controlled, comfortable, and narrated trolley tour ranging in length from an hour to most of the day on one of the specialty tours that gives you a glimpse of Lake View Cemetery, an understanding of the city in the '30s and '40s, and a

---

Why spend all day driving around in your vehicle looking for a parking spot when you can join a walking tour, a bike tour, or take a Segway tour of the city?

There are so many ways to explore Cleveland that don't include driving your own vehicle. Join one of the many walking tours or explore the city by bike, boat, or trolley. © Tonya Prater

look at Cleveland's ethnic neighborhoods.

Party Cycle Tours—Grab fifteen of your favorite people and take your party to the streets for some serious pedal action. This group bike ride will take you through some of Cleveland's most historic neighborhoods as you pedal along main streets and back alleys in search of some of the best pubs in Cleveland.

Boat Tours—Enjoy a narrated boat cruise along Cleveland's waterways as you sit back and watch the skyline while learning little-known facts about the city.

18 CLEVELAND VENUS

Why did Venus lose her head?

The Carl B. Stokes Courthouse may be the stunning gem of the Cleveland skyline, but its thirty-seven-foot-tall headless Venus standing sentinel at the courthouse entrance is the real star of the show.

The bronze beauty was sculpted by Jim Dine, an Ohio native, who is known for his Venus-inspired works of art, most notably the Venus of the Avenues in New York City.

In Cleveland, Dine took blind justice to a whole new level by intentionally removing the head of this Venus, which he said would take away any "implied narrative carried by recognizable features."*

Creating and setting this enormous sculpture was a two-year process. It began in the state of Washington, where 250 mold sections were cast and set in bronze. Each of those pieces was welded around a stainless-steel framework. The result was a 23,000-pound bronze behemoth that road-tripped via truck from Washington to Cleveland.

Upon arrival, a crane lifted Venus onto her permanent residence, where today she reflects a larger-than-life rendition of the original Venus de Milo, which can be seen at the Louvre Museum in Paris, France. The Cleveland Venus may lack her head, but she certainly turns visitors' heads as she presides over justice in an entirely new way.

Although inspired by the original Venus that resides at the Louvre in Paris, France, Cleveland's version didn't retain her head; however, she does retain the right to pass judgment on those who pass through her doors.
© Deb Thompson

CLEVELAND VENUS

WHAT Carl B. Stokes Courthouse

WHERE 801 W. Superior Ave.

COST Free

PRO TIP View more of Jim Dine's artwork at the Cleveland Museum of Art.

No need to head to Paris to see larger-than-life sculptures. Simply head to the courthouse for a look at a Venus de Milo inspired piece of art.

19 CLEVELAND'S FRANKLIN CASTLE

Is the Tiedemann House really haunted?

Rumors abound of voices echoing from empty rooms, visitors feeling cold spots, and sounds of crying children when no children are in the home. There are hushed whispers of hidden rooms and secret passageways. While any proof is still a ghostly figment, Franklin Castle (also known as the Tiedemann House) lends itself to a dark history that still haunts it today.

The original owner, Mr. Tiedemann, was a grocer and investment banker who was said to be a hard and loud man. During his reign in the home, his teen daughter passed away, then his mother, and, in the following three years, three more of his children. Soon, Mr. Tiedemann's wife, Luisa, succumbed to death as well.

Mr. Tiedemann didn't remain long in the home after his wife's passing, and the house stood empty until the late 1960s. That's when a family moved in and started reporting visits from the other side.

They were the first of many new owners. The castle that once stood stoic in a booming industrial city slowly took a beating from the elements of weather and time. This hulking gothic structure is now the story of rumors, ghosts, and murder. Yet hope remains as new owners try to build it back up to its former glory and, hopefully, once and for all, let the past remain in the past.

CLEVELAND'S FRANKLIN CASTLE

WHAT Franklin Castle

WHERE 4308 Franklin Blvd.

COST Free

PRO TIP No tours available, as the home is a permanent residence.

Built in 1881 for a prominent Cleveland family, the Franklin Castle has a sad and painful past and is said to have ghosts roaming its halls. © Deb Thompson

Stories of ghostly happenings at the Franklin Castle abound, but are they just stories or is something more sinister lurking in the shadows?

20 CURE YOUR CRAVINGS

How many ethnic foods can you find under one roof?

Step into Westside Market, Cleveland's oldest operating and municipally owned market, on any given week and you can almost instantly feel the atmosphere shift from that of outside. Your senses are instantly awakened by the endless aromas and constant shouting from the vendors trying to peddle their goods that fill the hall. "HOMEMADE CANNOLIS!" "GET YOUR BRATWURST HERE!" "EMPANADAS! WE HAVE EMPANADAS!" "TRY OUR BAKLAVA!"

A medley of flavors awaits you under this grand vaulted ceiling nestled in one of Cleveland's oldest neighborhoods, Ohio City. Patrons hustle and bustle about the stalls searching for the perfect ingredients, be it meats, breads, spices, herbs, sweets, or so much more, to make up or complement whatever meals they are planning for the week to come.

Westside Market consists of ninety-six vendors representing many of the 117 ethnic cultures that can be found in the Greater Cleveland area. While exploring the market, not only can patrons find great ingredients but they can also indulge in global delights prepared by the vendors, such as bratwurst, stuffed cabbages, potato pancakes, tamales, enchiladas, fresh pita, hummus, pizza bagels, or baklava, just to name a few. Of course, they also have regional favorites, such as pierogies, polish boys, and corned beef sandwiches.

CURE YOUR CRAVING

WHAT Westside Market

WHERE 1979 W. 25th St.

COST Free

PRO TIP Take the stairs to the balcony to get a bird's-eye view of the market.

The forty-four-foot-high Guastavino tile ceiling watches over the hustle and bustle below. Built in 1912, the ceiling is a highlight of any visit to the market.
© Deb Thompson

Those who are hungry for more than food will be tempted by the historical features of this 1912 building, including the 137-foot clock tower that greets customers at the front entrance and the forty-four-foot-high Guastavino tile ceiling that lords above the market activities.

Almost one hundred different food
vendors wait inside these walls to
tempt your taste buds and help
cure your cravings.

21 CUYAHOGA VALLEY NATIONAL PARK BEAVER MARSH

What creature transformed this dump into a nature lover's playground?

It's hard to imagine that the serene landscape of the Beaver Marsh in the Cuyahoga Valley Park was once a mass of gnarled, rusted, abandoned vehicles. The Beaver Marsh can be seen from the train or accessed via the Ohio & Erie Canal Towpath Trail. A popular spot for those visiting Ohio's only National Park, the wetlands area is designated an Important Bird Area by the National Audubon Society and is perhaps one of the best places to view beaver activity in the state of Ohio. It's also a great spot to see turtles, snakes, and various insects, a nature photographer's dream setting.

Prior to the National Park acquiring the land, the property the beaver marsh is located on was a dairy farm and, later, a junk yard until a plan was hatched in the 1980s to clean up and restore the property. Efforts were made by the Portage Trail Group, Sierra Club, National Park Service, and local community members, and the trash and debris were removed. But what happened next was nothing short of a miracle. Beavers, that were nearly extinct in Ohio, slowly came back to the area and made it their home.

CUYAHOGA VALLEY NATIONAL PARK BEAVERS MARSH

WHAT National Park

WHERE 3801 Riverview Rd., Peninsula

COST Free

PRO TIP Dusk offers the best chance of spotting beavers.

From trash to treasure: in less than forty years a public eyesore is transformed by beavers into one of the most popular and scenic areas of the Cuyahoga Valley National Park.
© Tonya Prater

They dammed the stream along the canal, and the rest is history. Those busy beavers are the reason so many visitors can enjoy the marsh from the train or along the trail to the boardwalk today.

An animal once near extinction was integral in the renewal of this marsh in Cuyahoga Valley National Park.

22 DON'T GO CHASING WATERFALLS

How many waterfalls can you find in the Greater Cleveland region?

It's hard to believe that the second largest city in Ohio is also home to a number of stunning waterfalls located throughout its extensive park system. Dotting the landscape, the waterfalls range from rather staid and boring to jaw-droppingly stunning. Hiking to them is a bit like unwrapping a gift, as you never know exactly what you'll find at the end of the trail. Impressive water displays depend entirely on the weather, with spring melt usually providing the most picturesque views.

Mill Creek Fall stands as the tallest waterfall within Cleveland, at forty-eight feet. The mile and a half hike to the falls ends in an impressive display of water falling over the rock as nature works hard at carving the landscape.

Take a short drive from Cleveland to the Cuyahoga Valley National Park and you'll discover the even more impressive Brandywine Falls, which has a sixty-five-foot drop into the gorge below. Upper and lower viewing platforms provide unique perspectives of the falls.

Lace up your hiking boots and head out on the trails to visit one or several of Cleveland's natural waterfalls.

Take a series of boardwalks and steps to Brandywine Falls, located in the Cuyahoga Valley National Park, and watch as the water cascades over a 65-foot drop. © Tonya Prater

Great Falls may not be as tall as the others but is still hike worthy, as the surrounding area provides an interesting landscape including the remains of an old mill.

Other notable waterfalls include Berea, Chagrin, and Buttermilk. For those willing to trek outside the city a bit, you'll find Paine, Stoney Brook Falls, East, and West falls.

DON'T GO CHASING WATERFALLS

WHAT Waterfalls

WHERE Various locations

COST Free

PRO TIP Most of Cleveland's waterfalls are easy to access and don't require a day-long hike.

ETERNAL EVER AFTER

What Lies Beneath?

Quietly walk among the tombstones of lives gone by, and make your way up the highest hill in the cemetery to the Garfield Memorial. This 180-foot-tall structure celebrates the life of President James A. Garfield, the 20th president of the United States and the second president to be assassinated while in office. Interestingly, President Garfield was hesitant to accept his party's nomination, and when he took office he sensed that he would never see his Ohio farm again. Sadly, the premonition came true.

As most cowardly assassinators are known to do, this one shot the president in the back while he was walking through a train station in Washington, DC. Sadly, it wasn't the bullet that ended President Garfield's life, but the blood poisoning that followed when doctors were unable to locate the bullet.

The grief-stricken public raised funds to build a memorial fit for a king, or president. The memorial that bears Garfield's name took eight years to build. It features a castle-like turret with circular stairs that lead to a large balcony that overlooks the cemetery and offers views of the city and, on a clear day, Lake Erie. That's how Lake View Cemetery got its name.

Lakeview Cemetery is a well-known tourist destination for good reason. Memorials, art, gorgeous landscapes, and lake views are a few reasons why people visit.

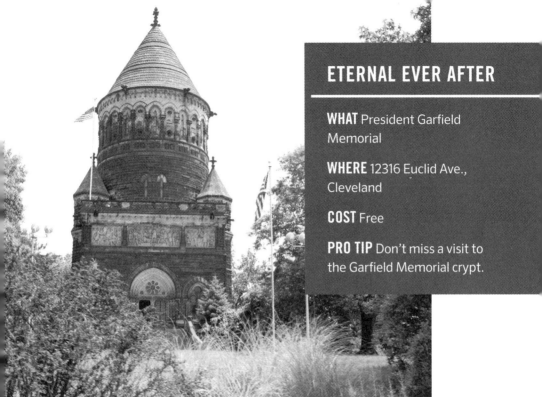

ETERNAL EVER AFTER

WHAT President Garfield
Memorial

WHERE 12316 Euclid Ave.,
Cleveland

COST Free

PRO TIP Don't miss a visit to
the Garfield Memorial crypt.

*A 180-foot-tall memorial pays homage to the 20th president of the
United States. The outside is impressive, but the inside is even more
so, with gorgeous mosaics, columns, and stained glass. Only those
who dare follow the stairs below ground. © Tonya Prater*

Inside the monument, no expense was spared. As
you walk around the memorial, you'll see gold mosaics,
columns, stained glass windows, and a larger-than-life-size
sculpture of President Garfield made of marble from the
same Italian quarries used by Leonardo da Vinci himself.
But it's what lies beneath this impressive memorial that
may send shivers down your spine.

If you dare, follow the marble staircase to the crypt
that lies below. Here, as your footsteps echo off the walls,
nothing stands between you and the 125-year-old coffin of
President Garfield, draped with an American flag. Next to
him lies his wife, who joined him in the eternal ever after
thirty-seven years later. Two urns that hold the ashes of his
daughter and son-in-law adorn a platform near the coffins.

24 FEDERAL RESERVE BANK OF CLEVELAND

Money doesn't grow on trees, or does it?

The Federal Reserve's job is to maintain a stable and strong banking system. There are twelve banks operated by the Federal Reserve located in various parts of the country that handle millions of dollars each day. Cleveland is home to one of those locations, and although the entire building is understandably not open to the public, the bank does operate a Money Museum. Designed to teach children how to properly handle their money so they can watch it grow, this onsite museum provides interactive exhibits to create a lasting impression.

Built in 1923 and listed on the National Registry of Historic Places, the Federal Reserve Bank of Cleveland Building is a stunning structure, with gorgeous marble, gold leaf, and painted ceilings. The building also houses the world's largest vault door in the world. The massive door is six feet thick and weighs over one hundred tons!

The Money Museum offers visitors an educational look at our monetary system. Visitors learn how to spot a counterfeit bill, make engravings with metal plates, design a dollar bill, put their face on a million dollar bill, and see

It's not very often that you can visit a museum and walk out with thousands of dollars in cash, but visitors to the Money Museum don't leave empty-handed.

Step inside the Federal Reserve Bank of Cleveland to travel back in time to learn the history of money, identify counterfeit bills, and watch money grow on a 23-foot-tall tree. © Deb Thompson

the different currencies used on American soil over the past two hundred years. Perhaps the best part of this museum is that it pays you to visit. That's right. Each guest to visit the Money Museum can leave with a bag of thousands of dollars of shredded money. Try not to spend it all in one place.

THE FEDERAL RESERVE BANK OF CLEVELAND

WHAT Museum

WHERE 1455 E. 6th St.

COST Free

PRO TIP Free public tours are offered Monday through Thursday from 9:30 a.m. to 2:30 p.m.

25 FLINTSTONE HOUSE

Is the flux capacitor broken again?

Fire up the DeLorean and set the date to 9,600 BC to get a glimpse of the Stone Age lifestyle. Peek into a world of cave dwellers and our very humble beginnings. No DeLorean? No worries. Simply go east from Cleveland until you come to Painesville to visit a modern-day take on Stone Age living. The home, settled low on the land, is almost easy to miss if you aren't watching closely. No, you didn't just pass through a time slip; you really are looking at a Stone Age style home.

Artist Wayne Trapp designed the cement dwelling in 1970 for the low cost of $30,000. The 3,400-square-foot house is, most likely, larger than most cave dwellings and is complete with five bedrooms, two bathrooms, and a hidden lookout nook.

Rounded exterior walls and roof make the home look like giant boulders have been strategically placed on the ground. The interior looks as if it were chiseled out of stone, complete with odd accents like upside down columns hanging from above, curving ceilings, uneven walls, a sunken tub, and even a sunken sitting area. The designer included built-in shelves, built-in reading nooks, and even built-in sleeping areas, with a tunnel connecting bedrooms.

Surprisingly, the design allows a significant amount of natural light to enter the home throughout the day, making it feel nothing at all like the Stone Age dwelling that inspired it.

FLINTSTONE HOUSE

Appearing as giant boulders that have been carved out to make a home, this Flintstone-esque property was built in 1970 and includes 3,400 square feet of living space and some really cool cave-like interior enhancements. © Deb Thompson

WHAT Flintstone House

WHERE 7245 Cascade Rd., Concord Township

COST Free

PRO TIP Drive 700 feet past the house to the bridge to see a waterfall.

No DeLorean required to visit a Stone Age inspired house that is referred to as the Flintstone House.

26 "FREE" STAMP

Do you know the history behind the World's Largest Rubber Stamp?

This giant replica of a rubber stamp may seem whimsical and quirky, but it may not be as light-hearted as it appears. One can't walk or drive past Willard Park, right outside Cleveland's City Hall in downtown Cleveland, without spotting the giant hand stamp lying on its side and emblazoned with the word "FREE" in capital (reversed) letters. Intriguing at best, this display of public art has an interesting backstory, as it was nearly destroyed by the very artist who first envisioned this piece that boasts the title "World's Largest 'Free' Stamp."

Commissioned by Standard Oil Company (SoHio), husband and wife duo Claes Oldenburg and Coosje van Bruggen were charged with the task of designing a piece of art to adorn the entrance to SoHio's new headquarters building, in 1982. Known for their larger-than-life and quirky statements of art, the duo designed the "Free" Stamp. But midway through the project, Standard Oil Company transitioned to BP America, and new management was convinced that the project would be derogatory for the company.

The sculpture was stored in a facility in Indiana until BP, tired of paying storage fees, pawned the piece of art off

---

Art is supposed to represent free speech, but this larger-than-life rubber stamp almost got scrapped for being too political.

"FREE" STAMP

If you've passed by City Hall, chances are you've spotted the controversial piece of art, but did you know the artist who created this giant sculpture once considered scrapping it? © Tonya Prater

WHAT Art installation

WHERE Corner of E. 9th St. and Lakeside Ave.

COST Free

PRO TIP The "Free" Stamp is only one of dozens of public art displays in downtown. Park in one of the nearby parking garages and explore downtown on foot for the best views.

on the city of Cleveland. The artists had selected what they felt was the perfect location for the stamp, on the lawn located beside City Hall, but public officials weren't sold on the idea until Coosje threatened to destroy the sculpture. The rest is history. Those passing by City Hall can now view the controversial piece of art on the corner of E. 9th St. and Lakeside Ave..

27

GET WELL SOON

How big is the Cleveland Clinic?

The clinic is almost ready to celebrate its 100th birthday and has been ranked the number one heart and heart surgery program in the United States since 1995. It is consistently listed as one of the top five hospitals in the country. It takes a lot of space to contain all this greatness, and the clinic could almost be classified as a city within a city. So large it has its own zip code!

The forty-four-building main campus stretches across almost 170 acres and averages over 6½ million patient visits a year. It has been on the cutting edge of medical procedures since the beginning. Some of its more famous breakthroughs include the first successful larynx transplant, the nation's first near-total face transplant, the discovery that adult brain neurons can regenerate, and the first kidney surgery performed through a patient's navel.

Beyond medical innovations, Cleveland Clinic incorporates the arts in their facility. Visual arts, music, performing arts, and a permanent art exhibit are enjoyed by patients and visitors alike. Twice a week, Art Ambassador Tours are offered that guide you around the temporary and permanent art exhibits. The collections of over 6,300 works of art are displayed in public spaces, hallways, and rooms.

Rated as the number one heart program in the United States, the Cleveland Clinic offers treatments for the soul as well as the body.

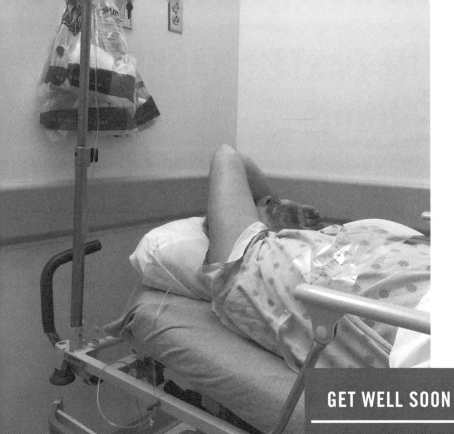

The Cleveland Clinic is one of the best medical facilities in the country, but in addition to curing the body, the Cleveland Clinic also offers an incredible collection of artwork displayed throughout its halls. © Deb Thompson

GET WELL SOON

WHAT Medical facility

WHERE 9500 Euclid Ave.

COST Free

PRO TIP Go to the top floor of the Sydell & Arnold Miller Pavilion for great views of downtown Cleveland.

28

GIANT EASTER BASKET IN LORAIN

Why build a giant Easter basket in the city?

Lorain lies approximately 30 miles west of Cleveland, along the Lake Erie Coastal Ohio Trail. The city boasts a restored lighthouse, historic rose garden, and the Charles Berry Bridge, which is the second largest bascule bridge in the world. In case you're wondering, bascule is simply a fancy word that most commonly refers to a drawbridge.

However, perhaps the best loved landmark in Lorain is the Giant Easter Basket that can be found at the opening of Lakeview Park. At seven feet tall by ten feet wide, the sizable concrete basket is not the largest basket in Ohio, but no doubt this basket shows up in more family photos than any other in the Buckeye State. The pastel-colored, woven concrete basket holds giant seventy-five-pound Easter eggs for the popular Christian holiday and has become the traditional background of choice for families over the years.

The basket was constructed in 1941 by Lorain Parks Department employee David Shukait, but the idea came from his boss, George Crehore, whose son requested a giant basket in the park. David went to work and not only created a hefty basket, he also patented the design.

A giant Easter basket built by a city employee in the city garage and moved to a public park for a community to enjoy for years to come.

Built to entertain one man's young son, this giant Easter basket has become an icon in the city of Lorain and an Easter tradition that generations will enjoy for years to come. © Deb Thompson

The Easter Basket was such a success that another, smaller basket was constructed for Oakwood Park, giving generations of residents a place to pose as a family or to take the ever-popular selfie.

GIANT EASTER BASKET IN LORAIN

WHAT Roadside attraction

WHERE 1800 W. Erie Ave., Lorain

COST Free

PRO TIP Don't make the trek simply to see the basket. While you're at the park, spend time exploring the rose garden and the lakeside.

29 GLASS BUBBLE PROJECT

Is this one of the hottest attractions in Cleveland?

Around the corner from the West Side Market in Ohio City is the Glass Bubble Project, an artisan studio that welcomes guests to try their hand, or should I say mouth, at the art of glassblowing. The building that houses the business is hard to miss. With a bright abstract mural painted on the side of the building, a door that is normally open, and a pet rooster named Morty II pecking away outside, this is one shop that nearly begs you to enter, and with ovens of molten glass, it just may be the hottest attraction in Cleveland.

Owner Mike Kaplan bought the property nearly twenty years ago when the area was less than desirable. He made a good purchase because Ohio City is now one of Cleveland's hot spots and success stories and so is Mike. Self-taught, you'll find his work at some of the top restaurants in the city. He also sells pieces to private individuals and businesses and now teaches classes to couples, scouts, school-age kids, and even team building for companies. Students can walk away with anything from a votive candle holder, to a shot glass, to an ice cream bowl, to wind chimes.

Mike grew up in a junkyard, so you'll find many of the projects created in the studio are made using recycled materials which includes metalwork in addition to the glasswork.

GLASS BUBBLE PROJECT

It's time to put your creativity to the test at the Glass Bubble Project in Ohio City. This learning studio specializes in glassblowing using recycled materials and offers classes to fit just about any need. © Tonya Prater

WHAT Business

WHERE 2421 Bridge Ave.

COST Free to look, classes vary

PRO TIP Pop in the studio for a free glassblowing demonstration.

One of Cleveland's hottest attractions can be found right around the corner from the iconic Westside Market in Ohio City.

What building in Cleveland boasts a priceless interior in honor of the dearly departed?

When it comes to professing your undying love and tying the knot surrounded by friends and family, an ornate chapel in the middle of Cleveland's most iconic cemeteries may not strike you as the perfect venue for a life ever after. Yet many couples have professed their everlasting love inside the lavish Wade Memorial Chapel, located in Lake View Cemetery. What makes this the idyllic spot to begin a life of love and passion? It's all about the glitz, baby.

While the exterior of the chapel resembles a Greek temple, one is unprepared for the beauty that lies within its bronze doors. That's right. The chapel features one of the few remaining interiors completely designed by Louis C. Tiffany, the son of Charles Tiffany, founder of the renowned Tiffany & Co. of New York.

The ornamental interior is exquisite from floor to ceiling and boasts white marble, bronze elements, glass mosaic wall panels, chandeliers, electric alabaster lights (among the first used in the city), and a priceless Tiffany stained-glass window that was displayed at the World Exposition in Paris in 1900. It's little wonder that Tiffany proclaimed the chapel as the work of his life.

By now you may be asking who deserved such an elaborate tribute? Jeptha Homer Wade wore many hats

HAPPILY EVER AFTER

WHAT Wade Chapel

WHERE 12316 Euclid Ave.

COST Free

PRO TIP A quick peek inside will leave you breathless, but plan to visit when you can join a tour to understand the symbolism in the chapel.

From the outside, Wade Chapel looks like many of the structures you'll find on the grounds of Lake View Cemetery, but that similarity ends when you step inside the bronze doors. © *Tonya Prater*

but is best known for his role as co-founder of Western Union Telegraph Company. He was very influential in the community, and his wealth was surpassed only by oil mogul John D. Rockefeller himself. A philanthropist, he gifted land to the city which is now part of the highly acclaimed University Circle. Jeptha Wade's grandson ordered the chapel to be built to honor his grandfather, who gave so much to the city of Cleveland.

Free tours of the chapel are available in season, April through November, but if you want to get hitched in this beauty, it will cost you some Benjamins.

A chapel built to honor the dearly departed becomes a popular venue for weddings.

31 HASEROT ANGEL

Have you ever seen an angel weep black tears?

Angels are commonly visible in cemeteries, adorning the graves of loved ones who have passed on. Often referred to as a messenger of God, angels may depict rebirth or resurrection. Less common is to find the Angel of Death presiding over a gravesite, but that's exactly what you'll find at Lake View Cemetery.

Unlike other angels, black tears stream down the cheeks and onto the neck of this notable bronze statue's face. Some say the "Angel of Death Victorious" that weeps over the gravesite of the Haserot Family while clutching an inverted torch, symbolizing a life extinguished or life in the next realm, is haunted. It may be, but I like to think that the tears streaming from the statue's murky eyes are more likely the result of discoloration from acid rain over the many years since it was created.

Francis Henry Haserot commissioned the notable sculptor Herman Matzen to design the Angel of Death effigy for his wife, Sarah, in 1923. The angel's gaze looks out over the family plot.

The exquisite and ornamental collection of cemetery sculptures located at Lake View Cemetery has earned the graveyard the unofficial title of "Outdoor Art Museum," with its collection of decorative crypts and funerary art. Sprawling nearly 300 acres with over 70,000 graves, the

If you get creeped out easily, plan to arrive during the day to see this hair-raising memorial and leave before dusk.

HASEROT ANGEL

WHAT Sculpture

WHERE 12316 Euclid Ave.

COST Free

PRO TIP The Haserot Angel can be found in Section 9, behind the Hanna Mausoleum.

Perhaps the most photographed memorial in Lake View Cemetery, the Haserot Angel that presides over the Haserot family plot appears to weep a stream of black tears from its hollow eyes. © Tonya Prater

necropolis almost reads like a Who's Who of Cleveland, with headstones prominently displaying the engraved names of Rockefeller, Hanna, Mather, Glidden, and Ness.

The cemetery may be a place of death, but it is also a place for the living. Visit, admire, and learn about the many lives that have made an impact on Cleveland over the past century. Visitors are welcome, and several group tours are also offered throughout the year that include a Lolly the Trolley tour on select summer weekends.

32 HEAD TO THE BEACH

Hey, are you sure we're not at the ocean?

Billions of grains of sand blanket the shore of Lake Erie, inviting beach lovers to her coast, which looks more like an ocean and less like a Great Lake. Sunbathers, beachcombers, and beach lovers all descend on Ohio's largest beach to absorb the sun and surf.

This mile-long beach east of Cleveland offers so much more than lying on the beach or playing in the water. There is fishing, boating, birding, and hiking through Headlands Dunes State Nature Preserve that adjoins the park. The Dunes, which are best viewed in the morning before the sand heats up, are home to several plant species that are also found along the Coast of the Atlantic.

The beach is unique in that part of the beach is groomed for sunbathers and swimmers, while the other half of the beach is left in its natural state, unkempt and strewn with driftwood. From here, you'll see the Fairport Harbor West Breakwater Lighthouse, which is situated near the break wall. Built in 1925 and listed on the National Register of Historic Places, this lighthouse was built at the mouth of the Grand River to replace the original lighthouse, which now serves as a maritime museum on a hill overlooking the lake.

The Fairport Harbor West Lighthouse has been uninhabited since 1948, but that could change. In 2011, it was purchased for the sum of $71,010 with the purpose of undertaking renovations to turn the property into a vacation retreat with incredible lake views. If that happens and you were to make reservations, make sure you pack light, as access to the lighthouse is via part of the mile-long sandy beach and across the break wall.

HEAD TO THE BEACH

WHAT State Park

WHERE 9601 Headlands Rd., Mentor

COST Free

PRO TIP The water quality is tested daily, and the results are posted on the large signs as you enter the parking lot.

Headlands Beach in Mentor is the longest beach in Ohio. The unkempt, natural appearance on part of the beach leads to the feeling that you're not on a Great Lake, but at the ocean. © Tonya Prater

This mile-long beach east of Cleveland will make you doubt that you're still in Ohio and haven't been transported to the Atlantic Ocean.

33 HEINEN'S FINE FOOD GROCERY STORE

Can shopping for groceries be a pleasant experience?

One doesn't expect to find a grocery store in downtown Cleveland, especially not one as sophisticated as Heinen's Fine Foods. Housed in the former 1908 Cleveland Trust Building, this is one attraction you'll want to visit even if you don't have grocery shopping to do. The interior is a feast for the eyes, with the granite facades, Corinthian columns, and original murals, but the highlight of this architectural gem is the exquisite stained-glass rotunda—a true masterpiece.

Unlike shopping at a big box store, Heinen's serves up class and prides itself on high-quality foods and amazing customer service. You can shop from a comprehensive selection of fresh fruits and juices, organic vegetables, whole food selections, and an extensive selection in the health food aisles. You'll also find lunch foods and bakery items prepared on-site as a great alternative to the downtown restaurants during the lunch hour.

So whether you need a shot of your favorite organic fair trade coffee from one of the talented baristas, need to grab lunch at the Global Grill, which features recipes inspired from around the world, or need to purchase your groceries

In 2015, Cleveland's oldest family-owned grocery store moved into the exquisite Cleveland Trust Building to offer a shopping experience like no other.

Heinen's Fine Foods is housed in the former 1908 Cleveland Trust Building. One of the many stunning architectural features is the original stained-glass rotunda. © Deb Thompson

HEINEN'S FINE FOOD GROCERY STORE

WHAT Grocery store

WHERE 900 Euclid Ave.

COST Free

PRO TIP Even if you don't need to shop for groceries, you should stop to check out this store.

for the week, Heinen's has you covered. And if the thought of grocery shopping is too much for you to take in, you can relax on the second-floor lounge area, where you can sip samples of wine from an extensive collection for the ultimate tasting experience. Who knew a visit to the grocery store could be such an enjoyable experience?

34

HISTORIC CHURCHES OF TREMONT

Where can you find the largest concentration of historic churches in America?

In the mid to late nineteenth century, many immigrants of Central and Eastern European descent were headed to Cleveland. They brought with them their culture and religious beliefs, which they desired to practice in their new home. That influence is still found today in the churches in and around Lincoln Park in Tremont. With their tall spires reaching toward heaven, onion domes with rich patinas, stained-glass windows, and other ornate touches, Tremont continues to boast the largest concentration of historic churches of any neighborhood in America. The places of worship are as diverse as the people who settled in Cleveland.

Some of our favorite churches include:

The Pilgrim Congregational Church, built in 1894, was the first church on the city's west side to have electricity. The church also owns a rare Farrand-Votey pipe organ, one of three known to exist in the United States. As if that wasn't cool enough, you'll find the organ flanked by two original Tiffany windows.

The world's largest concentration of historic churches can be found in Tremont, with their striking architectural features of domes, spires, and stained-glass touches.

Historic churches abound in the up-and-coming artsy community of Tremont. With a higher concentration of historical churches than any other neighborhood in the United States, Tremont prides itself on the holy structures. © Tonya Prater

THE HISTORIC CHURCHES OF TREMONT

WHAT Architecture

WHERE Tremont

COST Free

PRO TIP Park your vehicle at Lincoln Park and stroll through Tremont, viewing the architectural gems.

If you've watched *The Deer Hunter,* starring a young Robert De Niro and Christopher Walken, you've seen a glimpse of the St. Theodosius Cathedral, which is considered one of the finest examples of Russian church architecture in the United States. The imposing structure is lit up at night and can be seen for miles around.

Zion United Church of Christ, 1885, is noted for its 175-foot-tall steeple. Attended by a large German population, the church held services in German until 1916, when one English service was added to the roster each week. Sadly, due to declining membership and attendance, part of the church is being turned into apartments. The church will retain space on the property to hold services for its shrinking membership.

Take a stroll through the holy community of Tremont and admire the varied architecture of the historic churches.

35

HISTORIC KIRTLAND AND THE KIRTLAND TEMPLE

Do you know the beginnings of Mormonism can be found in Northeast Ohio?

Step back in time to the 1830s, when Ohio was yet a wilderness and the Church of Jesus Christ of Latter-Day Saints was in its infancy. It was in this settlement on the Chagrin River that Mormon leader Joseph Smith received visions from God that became integral in the formation of the church.

The bustling community named Kirtland flourished and became the location where many firsts for the religious sect have been attributed, which include the building of first LDS temple.

The Kirtland Temple is the only temple to survive that was attended by Joseph Smith. Built in the Federal style, the three-story building is also one of the only temples not to resemble the elaborate style of the Great Temple in Salt Lake City. At the time it was built, and during most of the nineteenth century, it was one of the largest buildings in Northeast Ohio.

Some of the buildings that were in the town of Historic Kirtland have been restored or

The Newell K. Whitney General Store in Historic Kirtland is a restored 1830s country store and post office stocked with thousands of items.
© Tonya Prater

recreated. These include a 10,000-square-foot visitors center, replicas of a one-room schoolhouse, ashery, sawmill, and John Johnson Inn, where church leaders were known to conduct business.

To Mormons, traveling to Northeast Ohio to Historic Kirtland is like traveling to Jerusalem for many Christians; it's part of a pilgrimage. Nearly two million visitors are drawn to Kirtland each year, in part to see the annual Historic Kirtland Nativity Exhibit that consists of more than 600 nativity scenes and over 100,000 outdoor lights, complete with Christmas music, and is recognized by the American Bus Association as one of the "Top 100 Events in North America."

The Church of Jesus Christ of the Latter-Day Saints got its start in Northeast Ohio in Kirtland, a small settlement. Here, devotees will find the first Mormon Temple ever built.

36 HISTORY OF CONTRACEPTION COLLECTION

What do pills, poison, and animal excrement all have in common?

Contraceptives have been much debated over the years, but one thing is agreed upon. Humans will go to great lengths to prevent pregnancy. Over the centuries amorous lovers have ingested everything from beaver testicles and crocodile excrement to poison. All told, hundreds of contraceptive methods have been attempted, most without any success. The fascinating array of contraceptive devices and written historical contraceptive ideas can be found on display at the Percy Skuy Collection on the History of Contraception.

Dr. Percy Skuy, a Canadian pharmacy executive, was drawn to collecting contraceptive methods and historical texts on the subject over more traditional objects of affection, like baseball cards or passport stamps. Over the years, he amassed more than six hundred ways to avoid contraception for his unconventional collection.

The extent that humans will take to prevent pregnancy has a long and interesting history that can be researched at the Percy Skuy History of Contraception exhibit.

Of all the collections you may see at a museum, the most unique may be this collection of contraceptive methods at the Dittrick Museum of Medical History. There are over 1,100 items on display.

HISTORY OF CONTRACEPTION

WHAT Museum

WHERE 11000 Euclid Ave.

COST Free

PRO TIP Located inside the Dittrick Museum of Medical History

The collection focuses on more than medical intervention. The collection includes ancient schemes as well as a handful of folkloric techniques and considers the religious influence on contraceptive practices.

In 2004, Dr. Skuy donated his entire collection to the Dittrick Medical Museum on the campus of Case Western Reserve University. After the collection moved to the university, more donations rolled in, and the total number of exhibit items now numbers well over 1,100.

This unique exhibit showcases the burning desire humans have to be intimate while impeding fertility. As you wander through the exhibit, you'll learn about pregnancy prevention from the past, present, and the future, but you may not want to try them all at home.

37 HO-HO-HO, MERRY CHRISTMAS

Are you ready for some holiday cheer?

Christmas lovers around the world unite and make plans to head to Medina, a short drive south of Cleveland, where Christmas never ends. Located an easy walk from town square, in a nondescript brick building, sits a place where every day of the year is a holly, jolly Christmas. This is America's largest indoor year-round Christmas entertainment attraction, Castle Noel.

Created by Mark Klaus, master sculptor and collector, in 2013, Castle Noel has quickly grown to be one of Medina's favorite attractions. Here, guests are encouraged to leave the frustrations of everyday life behind when they step through the doors and into a world that is adorned and wrapped in everything Christmas. Here you'll find the largest privately owned collection of Christmas movie props and costumes, from movies like *The Grinch, The Santa Clause, Elf,* and many more.

There is no need to head to the Big Apple during the holiday season to enjoy the spectacular animated window displays and lights. Simply head to Castle Noel, where you'll discover an impressive collection straight from Sak's Fifth Avenue, Bloomingdale's, Lord & Taylor, and Macy's in New York City.

Throughout the tour experience the Blizzard Vortex, Santa's Chimney Squeeze, indoor snowing, and go down the slide just like Ralphie from *A Christmas Story*.

It is Christmas year-round at Castle Noel. Hollywood sets, movie costumes, and window displays from New York City now have a new home at this attraction in Medina. © Tonya Prater

HO-HO-HO, MERRY CHRISTMAS

WHAT Attraction

WHERE 260 S. Court St., Medina

COST $17

PRO TIP Stop in the gift shop to pick up a hand-crafted sculpture by Mark Klaus.

Experience holiday cheer all year long at Castle Noel, America's largest indoor year-round Christmas entertainment attraction.

HOLLYWOOD IN THE CITY

What Hollywood stars shine across Cleveland?

Some of the biggest Hollywood blockbuster movies can thank Cleveland for providing epic backdrops for their scenes. Cityscapes, downtown buildings, department stores, orchestra halls, museums, and even area restaurants can all be spotted throughout numerous films.

Walk where some of your favorite movie stars have walked and visit locations straight from your favorite movies. Cult classics such as *A Christmas Story* and *The Deer Hunter* may have helped direct Hollywood's eye to Cleveland's photogenic nature. *A Christmas Story* is so popular that the house used for filming is open for public tours, as is the Russian Orthodox Church from *The Deer Hunter*. Both are a must-see for any visiting film enthusiasts.

More current films include *The Fate of the Furious, Air Force One, The Avengers, Captain America: Winter Soldier, Spider-Man 3, American Splendor, Alex Cross*, and *Jenny's Wedding*.

Marvel spent considerable time in the city for the filming of *The Avengers* and *Captain America* and managed to include many of Cleveland's iconic landmarks in the two films. The lower viaduct on the Detroit-Superior Bridge, Public Square with Tower City in the background, East 9th Street, the glass-enclosed atrium at the Cleveland Museum of Art, the West Shoreway, and the inside of Tower City. Though the films may claim they are somewhere else entirely, all these Cleveland-based locations made an appearance.

In addition to the spots mentioned above, other popular filming locations include Severance Hall, Cleveland City Hall, Case Western Reserve University, and Euclid Ave.

HOLLYWOOD IN CLEVELAND

WHAT Filming locations

WHERE Various spots

COST Free

PRO TIP Follow the Cleveland Film Facebook page to stay up-to-date on all the Hollywood happenings in the city.

Cleveland has become a hotspot for movie filming. Tower City and the adjacent public park make many appearances in Hollywood films. Everything from Marvel's The Avengers *to* Captain America *have used this iconic backdrop in their blockbuster hits.*
© Deb Thompson

Cleveland continues to be on Hollywood's radar, as filming in the area seems to be relentless. Upcoming films from A-listers like Bruce Willis and Matthew McConaughey all have filming under way.

No need to purchase an airline ticket to Hollywood to indulge in movie sets and movie stars. Simply head to hot spots around Cleveland to watch Hollywood in action.

39 THE HOUSE OF WILLS

Can this property be saved?

Even in its current deteriorated condition, passersby of the former House of Wills Funeral Home on E. 55th St. can see evidence that the now dilapidated structure was once a building of beauty. Above the door on the front of the building, the proud HOUSE OF WILLS sign remains over the double doors, proclaiming that the three-story architectural wonder is indeed something special.

Designed and built by notable Cleveland architect Frederick W. Striebinger in 1905, the property has had a colorful past. Originally it served as a German social club, followed by a hospital, a speakeasy during Prohibition, and as headquarters for the Civil Rights Movement in Cleveland. As a funeral home, the House of Wills was one of the most successful black businesses in Cleveland and reported to be the largest black funeral home in the state.

Serving both the living and the dead, the funeral home served double duty as a location for social functions for African Americans as well. The interior of the home boasted many striking features that include impressive decorative moldings that simply aren't found in homes that are built today.

A once gorgeous funeral home from the early twentieth century has fallen prey to thieves and vandals since it was abandoned in 2005.

Passing by on 55th St., it's difficult hard to imagine the splendor that this stately property, that served as a funeral home, exhibited. ©Tonya Prater

THE HOUSE OF WILLS

WHAT Architecture

WHERE 2491 E. 55th St.

COST Free

PRO TIP This is private property, but tours are offered several times a year or by contacting the owner to schedule one.

The building was abandoned in 2005, when it fell prey to thieves and vandals. The current owner, Eric Freeman, saved the property from what was sure to be demolition and has big plans to renovate the property into usable space.

The gorgeous architecture is not all that remains in this historic property. It is rumored that the space is a hub for paranormal activity and is a popular destination for ghost hunters.

40 INSTAGRAMMABLE PLACES

Where will you take a selfie?

Make sure your cell phone is fully charged and you have your best face on because selfie opportunities abound around the streets of Cleveland. Pay close attention while driving around and you'll spot incredible murals, cool graffiti, and noteworthy landmarks. Once you find a spot that calls out to you, stopping for a selfie is a must. Some places will require a bit of patience while searching for parking, but the memorable upload to Instagram will make it worth the effort.

Stop at the corner of 25th and Chatham St. and stand in front of the Greetings from Cleveland mural. Each letter in CLEVELAND tells a story about the city. Painted within the letter outlines are famous city landmarks and sports icons. Its colorful explosion of art on an otherwise boring city wall sums up the city history in nine letters.

Want a selfie with the fabulous skyline instead? Search out one of the three Cleveland script signs that are located at Edgewater Park, 1001 E. 9th St. in the North Coast Harbor, and 1430 Abbey Ave. in the Tremont neighborhood. The enormous signs stand six feet high and sixteen feet long and are sure to make your photos pop.

Two other famous selfie spots include the largest street chandelier, located in the theater district, and in front of the one and only Rock and Roll Hall of Fame.

Regardless of where you are in the city, you are sure to find your perfect Instagrammable moment.

This Cleveland mural, in the Ohio City neighborhood, showcases all the things that Cleveland is famous is for within its letters. Created by Greetings Tour, it is the perfect location to take an Instagrammable-worthy photo. © Deb Thompson

INSTAGRAMMABLE PLACES

WHAT Public art

WHERE 2098 W. 25th St. and 1502 Abbey Ave.

COST Free

PRO TIP Street parking near Westside Market

Selfie spots abound in this Rust Belt city, with numerous, photo-worthy locations.

41

INTERNATIONAL WOMEN'S AIR & SPACE MUSEUM

What role have women played in the history of aviation?

Tucked inside the terminal of Burke Lakefront Airport is a museum few people know about. For thirty years, the International Women's Air & Space Museum has been sharing the role that women have served in aviation history. You'll find memorabilia and historical artifacts that have been accumulated and protected by the Ninety-Nines, the international organization of women pilots that was formed in 1929 with ninety-nine charter members. Amelia Earhart served as its first president, in 1931.

Exhibits and collections in the museum educate the public on a variety of subjects—from WASP, the Women Airforce Service Pilots who collectively flew over 60 million miles during World War II, to the Mercury testing program and work with NASA, to women achieving the goal of becoming a commercial pilot. You'll see the stories of Amelia Earhart, the first woman to fly solo across the Atlantic Ocean, and of Sally Ride, the first American woman

This small but mighty gem features displays that honor women who have made an impact in the air and space industry.

INTERNATIONAL WOMEN'S AIR & SPACE MUSEUM

WHAT Museum

WHERE 1501 N. Marginal Rd.

COST Free

PRO TIP Enhance your visit with the free audio tour that can be accessed via your cell phone.

If you've flown into the Cleveland Burke Lakefront Airport, you may have noticed the exhibits that line the hallway that pay homage to great women in the flight and space industry. ©Tonya Prater

to fly in space, unfold throughout the exhibits and learn about some of the lesser known accomplishments by women throughout Northeast Ohio and throughout the world.

The museum and parking are free to visitors and school groups, scouts, and birthday parties to explore and learn about the significant role women have played in aviation history.

42

INVENTION OF POTATO CHIP MANUFACTURING

Can you eat just one?

It's America's favorite salty snack food, with over a billion pounds being consumed annually. Americans everywhere can thank George Crum for creating the crispy, salty goodness that is a potato chip. However, we really need to thank William Tappenden of Cleveland for bringing this popular snack to the masses.

Prior to 1895, potato chips were only consumed in restaurants. Mr. Tappenden was the first individual to peel, fry, salt, and package potato chips in his small home kitchen and deliver them to local stores via horse and buggy. The snack grew in popularity, and he soon outgrew his home kitchen and converted part of his barn to a potato chip processing facility. His efforts are recognized as being one of the first potato chip factories in the country.

The potato chip making process was time consuming. Each potato had to be hand peeled and hand sliced, one potato at a time, until there were enough to fry up and sell to area grocers. Due to this, the potato chip was largely a regional food item.

It wasn't until the 1920s that an automated potato peeler was invented and potato chips jumped to the number one spot on the snack chart. This invention birthed three large potato chip companies: Wise Potato Chips, Lay's Brand Potato Chips, and Utz Hanover Home Brand Potato Chips. Oddly enough, Mr. Tappenden falls off the history books after the invention of the automatic potato peeler, but his legacy remains with each crispy bite taken across the U.S. of A.

Potato chips may have been created by a chef in Maine, but we have a savvy inventor and businessman from the Cleveland area to thank for bringing these salty, crispy bites to the masses. © Deb Thompson

CAN YOU EAT JUST ONE?

WHAT Invention of potato chip manufacturing

WHERE Cleveland

COST Free

PRO TIP N/A

It's America's favorite snack, and a Cleveland native is credited with starting one of the first potato chip factories in the country. Thanks Mr. Tappenden!

43 IT'S A BIRD, IT'S A PLANE, IT'S SUPERMAN!

Are you faster than a speeding bullet?

Drive down a nondescript street in the Glenville neighborhood, and you'll pass by the "American dream" of a house with the white picket fence and 2.5 kids. However, instead of the 2.5 kids, this is the birthplace of Superman, the lovable hero from Krypton who plummeted to Earth when his planet was dying.

Known as being faster than a speeding bullet and able to leap tall buildings in a single bound, fans of one of America's favorite comic book heroes can visit the homes where inspiration struck and magic happened. Superman was born from Jerry Siegel's imagination while Joe Shuster brought him to life through his drawings. Together, in 1932, they created one of the most iconic fictional characters of the twentieth century.

However, creating the most popular character of the century didn't guarantee a fortune-filled life. The duo sold their creation to DC Comics in 1938 for a mere $130. DC Comics held all rights to the superhero, leaving Siegel and Shuster out in the cold with no royalties or benefits. They took odd jobs to support themselves

IT'S A BIRD, IT'S A PLANE, IT'S SUPERMAN!

WHAT Historical location

WHERE Corner of Amor Ave. and Parkwood Dr.

COST Free

PRO TIP Be sure to visit the historical marker honoring them at a nearby park at the northeast corner of E. 105th St. and St. Clair Ave./ Hwy 283.

At the corner of Amor Ave. and Parkwood Dr. you'll find the home of Joe Schuster, one of the creative geniuses behind the iconic Superman comic. Storyboards line the property for visitors to enjoy. © Deb Thompson

until 1975, when they sued DC Comics and a settlement in their favor netted them $20,000 per year each for the rest of their lives plus credit. Even with the settlement, they would each only earn roughly $400,000 for their multi-million-dollar creation.

Today, Superman aficionados can visit Joe Schuster's house and see where the magic happened while reading comic strip boards lining the property.

One of America's most iconic super heroes, Superman, was born in the small Glenville neighborhood where two neighbors created this famous comic strip.

44 IT'S A PLETHORA OF FESTIVALS

What are you doing this weekend?

One thing that Clevelanders are never allowed to say is that they are bored. The city is replete with fun-filled activities almost every day of the year. If there isn't a major-league sports game, a theater production, or museum event happening, there is definitely a festival going on to join. Hundreds of fairs and festivals take place, ensuring that the residents of this great city always have something to do.

There are the standard festivals that celebrate music of all types, food, wine, beer, and art.

Of course, this is Cleveland, so in addition to the main street festivals that fill the city's event calendar, there are more unique festivals to pique your curiosity. From cultural, ethnic, and street festivals to everything in between, you are sure to find a new reason to celebrate.

Some of the more "interesting" festivals include:
- Duck Tape Festival—celebrating the "fix-it" master
- Tater Tot and Beer Festival—the title says it all
- Chalk Festival—grab your chalk and get ready to make chalk art
- Twin Day Festival—celebrating everything twins
- National Hamburger Festival—find the craziest burger combos
- Garlic Festival—because why not?
- Dyngus Day—a Polish festival to end all Polish festivals

This is definitely a city that lets you shake off the traditional and indulge in the unusual.

There is never a reason to be bored in this Rust Belt city. There are hundreds of festivals, fairs, and cultural events happening in the region throughout the year, including the one-of-a-kind Duck Tape Festival. © Deb Thompson

IT'S A PLETHORA OF FESTIVALS

WHAT Entertainment

WHERE Various locations

COST Varies

PRO TIP Summer provides the most bang for your buck when it comes to the number of festivals happening each weekend.

Dust off your party shoes and take in one of the hundreds of fun festivals held in the region every year.

CURE YOUR CRAVINGS (page 40)

Margaret J. Postgate (1879-1953)

Margaret Postgate was born in Chicago, Illinois to English parents who had immigrated to the United States just a few years prior. Her father was a newspaper man who worked for a time at the *Chicago Evening Post* and while the family was living there, Margaret attended the Art Institute of Chicago to study drawing and painting. When her father's career took the Postgates to New York City, she continued her studies at the Art Students League and the Cooper Union.

Postgate became best known for her work as a fine art sculptor and for her promotional soap sculptures on behalf of the Procter and Gamble Company. P&G held annual national Ivory Soap carving contests to promote the product, and Postgate won the competition in 1924 with one of three elephant carvings she submitted. P&G sent the soap carvings on tour and exhibitions stopped at both the Cleveland Museum of Art and the 1927 Art in Industry Exposition at Halle Brothers in downtown Cleveland. Postgate herself was also asked by P&G to visit tradeshows and do soap carving demonstrations as well as design how-to brochures on the subject. Along the way, her work was discovered by R. Guy Cowan.

All of Margaret Postgate's designs for Cowan Pottery are believed to have originated as soap sculptures. She did visit the Rocky River studios in 1928, but worked out of Brooklyn, New York and sent her designs to Cowan where they were put into production. In 1929, she modeled the angular, modernistic elephant that would become the two sets of bookends seen here. Postgate's most successful Cowan sculpture was the rounded *Elephant* from 1930 that was produced as a large limited edition sculpture, a set of bookends, and a smaller format paperweight.

Postgate produced a number of religious sculptures. *The Three Marys* depicts Mary Magdalene, Mary the mother of Jesus, and Mary the sister of Martha in a small but moving sculpture. The curving form of Mary is repeated in small patinated brass sculpture that was then produced as a larger version for Cowan. Her *Modern Madonna* presents a highly stylized Mary, with the head of the baby Jesus just visible in her arms.

Following her brief but successful [...] h Cowan, Postgate continued to cr[...] he also worked in sculpted por[...] n. She was a long-time [...] r of 1953.

IVORY

MO[...]
S[...]
SCUL[...]
in
By Mar[...]

ALL THAT JAZZ (page 12)

BRIDGE TO NOWHERE (page 26)

THE BOOKBINDER

Revised
&
Expanded

The Used Book Lover's Guide to the Midwest

Book Hunter Press

JOHN DUNNING

THE BOOKWOMAN'S LAST FLING

SCRIBNER

knitter's stash

ALBRIGHT

JANE
AUSTEN
❦
PRIDE AND
PREJUDICE

FOLIO
SOCIETY

FREEMAN

Corduroy

WEEKLY READER BOOKS

LOGANBERRY BOOKS MURAL (page 124)

THAT'S A WRAP (page 166)

A WALK IN THE WOODS (page 8)

PAINT THE TOWN (page 136)

DAVIDSHILLINGLAW

CLEVELAND PUBLIC LIBRARY (page 32)

OUR LADY OF LOURDES SHRINE (page 134)

VISIT THE FOUR CONTINENTS (page 186)

IRELAND LOBBY

ETERNAL EVER AFTER (page 46)

HEAD TO THE BEACH (page 64)

45 JOHN HEISMAN'S BIRTHPLACE

Is this really where John Heisman was born?

The Heisman Trophy is one of the most coveted awards in college sports. Each year a few good men are hand-picked as the best of the best, and one of them walks away as the top dog. It's a bit like a Miss America pageant, but replace girls in bikinis with guys in football gear. Every December this trophy is awarded to a college football player who is outstanding in his athleticism, performance, and integrity.

Many don't know the man for whom the trophy is named. That gentleman is John W. Heisman. Taking his first breath in 1869 in an industrial midwestern town on the edge of Lake Erie, he was born in a humble house on a tree-lined street. Sometime after his birth, his parents relocated to Pennsylvania, where he played football.

After high school, Mr. Heisman went on to become an innovator and pioneer of the game of football as well as a superior coach. It's him we have to thank for how the game is played today. Forward pass, center snap, "hike" the ball to start the play, and dividing the game into quarters are the result of Mr. Heisman.

Thirty years ago, a historical marker was erected in front of a home to commemorate the birthplace of John Heisman.

HEISMAN BIRTHPLACE HISTORICAL MARKER

WHAT John W. Heisman Birthplace historical marker

WHERE Bridge St. and W. 29th St.

COST Free

PRO TIP Be sure to see what some historians consider the actual house, at 3928 Bridge St.

A historical marker about John Heisman, for whom the Heisman Trophy is named, was placed in front of a two-story, shabby house where some say he was born. © Deb Thompson

However, rumors abound that the marker is in front of the wrong house and that the actual birthplace of Heisman is about a half a mile down the street. The error resulted from houses being renumbered and a lack of fact checking. However, fans can still get a feel for the area and, if they wish, visit both the historical marker site and the site of what research shows to be the real birthplace of Heisman.

Regardless, Clevelanders can take pride in the fact that the Heisman Trophy got its start in their town.

John Heisman, the name behind the world-renowned college football trophy and all around football pioneer, took his first breath in Cleveland.

46

KABOOM

How many bombs does it take to blow up an Irishman?

How many detonated car bombs does it take to dub a city Car Bomb, U.S.A.? Cleveland can tell you the magic number is 36. Once a battlefield for the underbelly operations of the mob, Cleveland has few visible reminders of that 1970s crime spree, and no player seems to be more infamous as proud Irishman Danny Greene.

Danny seemed to have nine lives and survived four murder attempts, including one that took place at his home and office located at 15805 Waterloo Rd., when a bomb blast nearly leveled the property in 1975. Greene and his young girlfriend, who had been sleeping on the second floor of the building, miraculously survived, which Danny attributed to the "luck of the Irish." The lot where the building stood remains vacant today. It's in this lot that you'll find the KABOOM mural, part of the Waterloo Walls Project to kick off a beautification and rejuvenation of the Collinwood district.

Danny's death spurred a crackdown on crime in the city and twenty-two people were charged in connection with his murder. His life also inspired the book *To Kill the Irishman: The War that Crippled the Mafia* by author and longtime police officer Rick Porrello. The book later became a movie, *Kill the Irishman,* starring heavy hitters Ray Stevenson, Christopher Walken, and Vincent D'Onofrio. Surprisingly, the movie was not filmed in Cleveland, but in Detroit.

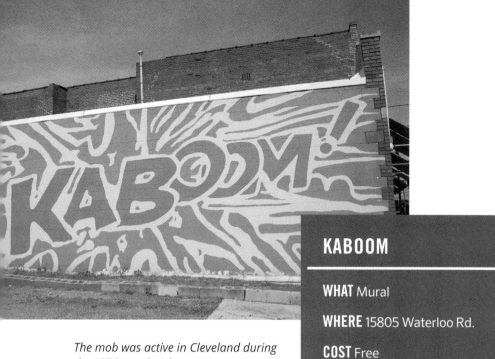

The mob was active in Cleveland during the 1970s, and Irishman Danny Greene was perhaps one of the most notorious players in the war that raged on the city's streets. © Tonya Prater

KABOOM

WHAT Mural

WHERE 15805 Waterloo Rd.

COST Free

PRO TIP Park in one of the public lots and walk down Waterloo Rd. to reach this mural.

The mob was active in Cleveland during the 1970s, and a handful of key players fought for control.

47

LAKE ERIE SALT MINES

What lies beneath Lake Erie?

Two miles under Lake Erie and four miles out, near Whiskey Island, a fleet of mineworkers don uniforms of hard hats and headlamps and set out to harvest salt from the depths of the earth. Those above the mines in Lake Erie have no idea what is taking place—not under the surface of the water, but under the lake itself. Workers drill holes into a layer of salt, dig away a passage about ten feet deep and lay explosives which detonate electronically at the end of the day. Above ground, the blast is undetectable.

The salt is then collected, scooped on a beltline, and brought to the surface using a series of conveyor belts and elevators. Engineers on-site calculate how many salt pillars should remain to support the ceiling of the mine.

Salt is plentiful under a layer of shale and limestone in Ohio because it is thought that Ohio was once under a shallow sea. The waters receded or evaporated, leaving behind a layer of salt 1,700 feet beneath the surface. Surprisingly, Lake Erie, the shallowest of the Great Lakes, is a mere fifty-six feet deep on average.

The salt that is collected in the Whiskey Island mine is used as a deicer to aid in safer driving conditions during the snowy, icy season. In 2015, the United States used over 17 million tons of rock salt on back roads, state

LAKE ERIE SALT MINES

WHAT Industry

WHERE Under Lake Erie

COST Free

PRO TIP The general population is unable to visit the salt mines.

Nearly two miles under the surface of Lake Erie, miners are hard at work harvesting salt to ensure we stay safe on ice and snow covered roads during the winter months. ©Tonya Prater

routes, and interstates. During a mild winter, the Cleveland mine operated by Cargill Deicing Technology generates 3 million tons of salt. If the winter is a little harsher, that number rises to 4 million. Next time you jump in your car during a snowstorm, you can thank an Ohio miner for their help to keep the roads clear.

Many Clevelanders have no idea that explosive blasts are a regular occurrence nearly two miles under Lake Erie.

48

LAND OF THE WARRES

Does a door to a parallel universe exist in Cleveland?

What if there were a world that exists in a universe that runs parallel to ours? What if the story of that universe is being told, a page at a time, on bronze plaques installed around the world, and to learn more about this universe you simply needed to find the plaques and read each page?

The fictional world of the Kcymaerxthaere Universe was created by Eames Demetrios, who is placing markers, aka pages, all around the world in locations where his fictional world is said to intersect with our reality. This project has been ongoing for more than ten years. Currently, eighty-three tiles have been placed in fifteen countries and five continents. The goal of the alternate reality inventor is to install 1,000 plaques across the globe.

The only door in Ohio to the Kcymaerxthaere Universe is located in Cleveland Heights on Perkins St. The metal plaque is attached to the corner of a brick building in a rough and tumble industrial area. It's easy to miss if not searching for this Land of the Warres plaque, which was installed in 2006. This page of the story tells the tale of beings, called Warres, who are described as "organisms that prefer shallow waters, best known for being a creature without metabolism."

LAND OF THE WARRES

WHAT Plaque

WHERE 4701 Perkins St.

COST Free

PRO TIP Cleveland is the only location in Ohio to have a "door" to this parallel world.

In a ramshackle, industrial part of town there is an unassuming brick building that is said to be a door to the Kcymaerxthaere Universe, a fictional world with storyboards around the globe. © Deb Thompson

Enter the fictional Kcymaerxthaere Universe by searching for and finding story plaques that have been strategically placed around the globe.

49

LET NATURE PAVE THE WAY

What is Cleveland's shortest street made of?

Heaven may have streets paved with gold, and history may have streets paved with brick, but Cleveland is home to a street paved with wooden blocks. Hessler Court, the shortest street in Cleveland, is a mere sixty yards long. It has been paved with wood bricks since the early 1900s and stretches from Hessler Rd. to Bellflower Ave. Other wood roads were eventually paved over with brick, pavement, or asphalt, but Hessler Court has maintained its original style of paving for over one hundred years.

Named after Emery Hessler, a surgical instrument salesman who owned the land, it is thought that Hessler Court was paved with wooden bricks around 1916. Nineteen thousand pieces of wood surface this short stretch. It may have been intended as a driveway to the Hessler home, but history remains fuzzy not only about when it was installed but why it was constructed. Regardless, the wooden street remains as it originally began, never to be replaced with more contemporary materials.

Hessler Court may not be the shortest street in Ohio, but it is the only remaining wood block paved road in the state. Since 1973, it has been listed on the National Register of Historic Places.

Paved in 1916 with wooden blocks, this short street continues to be the only street in Ohio paved with wood.

LET NATURE PAVE THE WAY

This may not be the shortest street in Ohio, but it's the only street that is still paved with wooden blocks. Hessler Court, located in University Circle, is still used for car traffic today. © Deb Thompson

WHAT Unique paving material

WHERE Located between Hessler Rd. and Bellflower Ave.

COST Free

PRO TIP Mitchell St. in Bellefontaine, a mere fifteen feet long, holds the record for shortest street in the world.

50

LET'S TAKE A SPIN

Are you brave enough?

Every year, like clockwork, the I-X Convention Center opens its doors to children and adults alike for the largest family friendly springtime event in the region. People from all over the country come to experience the twenty-plus acres of rides, games, food, and attractions. Including the I-X's main attraction, the Big Kahuna, Ohio's tallest indoor Ferris wheel.

Standing at an impressive 125 feet high, the top of the wheel protrudes 35 feet above the roof and is enclosed by a glass atrium. This permanent, awe-inspiring addition to the I-X Convention Center made its debut, oddly enough, at the 1992 Greater Cleveland Auto Show.

The best chance to take a spin on the Ferris wheel is during the I-X Indoor Amusement Park or during one of the handful of consumer shows. Sadly, the wheel doesn't turn during trade shows. The amusement park runs for two weeks each spring and is when the Ferris wheel makes the most rotations—some150,000 people pass through the doors during this epic two-week event.

Today, the wheel continues to draw visitors from around the region for a chance to ride what was once the world's largest indoor Ferris wheel.

Hope you're not scared of heights because this impressive Ferris wheel is so tall they had to remove part of the roof.

LET'S TAKE A SPIN

WHAT Indoor Ferris wheel

WHERE One I-X Center Dr.

COST Varies depending on event

PRO TIP Be sure to have your eyes open as you pass through the glass atrium at the top for great views of Downtown Cleveland.

Go up, up, and through the roof at one of the largest indoor Ferris wheels in the world. This is a one of a kind opportunity that you won't find in very many places around the world. Go through the roof and you're granted excellent views of downtown Cleveland. © I-X Center

119

51

LITERARY CLEVELAND

Do you have the write stuff?

Cleveland seems to be a cultural mecca. The city has everything from top-notch theaters, a world-renowned orchestra, award-winning museums, and three major sports teams. It's a given that a city holding all that greatness is also going to birth some famous authors along the way and put Cleveland on the map for its literary genius.

Cleveland has given life to the comic creators of *Calvin & Hobbes, Superman, American Splendor,* and *Ultimate Spider-Man* as well as many others.

Topping the author list is Toni Morrison, a Nobel Prize winner; Rita Dove, a Poet Laureate; and Dan Chaon, a popular young novelist and short story writer. Of course, it's impossible to talk about Cleveland authors without including John O'Brian (*Leaving Las Vegas*), Les Robers (Milan Jacovich series), and Thrity Umrigar (*The Space Between Us*).

In addition to famous authors, there are a number of famous books that are set within Cleveland, including *Crooked River Burning* by Mark Winegardner, the Milan Jacovich series by Les Roberts, *The Dead Key* by D.M. Pulley, and *The Broom of the System* by David Foster Wallace.

The extensive list of written works coming out of or based in Cleveland means that the city can add a literary notch to its cultural belt.

LITERARY CLEVELAND

WHAT Famous authors and books

WHERE Various locations

COST Free

PRO TIP Stop by Loganberry Books to pick up the latest story by one of Cleveland's own.

Reading addicts take note. Cleveland is a mecca of famous authors and Cleveland-based stories. In addition to great works of fiction and nonfiction, some of America's greatest comics were born in Cleveland, including Superman *and* Calvin & Hobbes. © Deb Thompson

Cleveland can lay claim to a number of famous cartoonists, authors, and books, including the creators of Superman, award-winning novelists, and more.

52

LITTLE FREE LIBRARIES

Is this the end of library fines?

Watch out Carnegie! There's a new library in town—well, nearly a hundred new libraries, that is. What began along homes, shops, and a bike trail in Wisconsin in 2009 has spread not only across the country but around the world. The Little Free Library is a grassroots crusade to foster community through the love of reading and does so by making books free for both children and adults at the tiny libraries found in communities throughout the world.

Cleveland is home to over eighty-five Little Free Libraries, and that number continues to grow. Located near schools, libraries (ironic, I know), and police stations, to name a few, these free-standing wooden boxes come in all shapes and sizes. One, a tiny replica of Doctor Who's TARDIS, located at 1378 Ardoon St., may be the most unique that I found in the city.

I also found the nearby Spirit Corner Little Free Library to be intriguing. Located on the site of a home that was abandoned for sixty years and thought by many neighborhood children to be haunted, Spirit Corner has been transformed into a beautiful park for the neighborhood to enjoy, after the razing of the home. With seating in the form of logs, boulders, and stone benches, perhaps the highlight of this park, located on the corner of Hampshire and Cadwell in Cleveland's historic Mayfield Heights district, is the Little Free Library that is stocked full of reading material. So if you're up for a little adventure and you're not scared away by ghosts, make your way to this charming park for a frightfully fun day.

LITTLE FREE LIBRARIES

WHAT Literary attraction

WHERE Varies

COST Free

PRO TIP The Little Free Libraries work off the premise that visitors will leave a book when they take one.

While Little Free Libraries can be found all over Cleveland in various shapes and sizes, the Dr. Who TARDIS, located on Ardoon St., is sure to transport you to another world. © Tonya Prater

If you're going to check out a book from a Little Free Library, remember to leave one in exchange. The libraries operate on the take one, leave one policy to continue to be successful.

Little Free Libraries are popping up all over Cleveland, transporting residents back in time and to another world.

53 LOGANBERRY BOOKS MURAL

Have you read these larger-than-life books?

Step inside a world of comfy chairs, floor-to-ceiling book shelves that offer up a diverse array of topics, cozy nooks, and a smell that only bookstores can provide. Breathe deep and let your gaze roam over the thousands of books that are new, used, and rare as you plot your adventure through the tales. People may come to Loganberry Books for the atmosphere and selection, but there remains a larger-than-life reason to visit.

Once you have quenched your literary thirst, exit the store and make a left and then make another left at the end of the building and walk into the small courtyard. You may do a double-take to make sure you didn't just step through the looking glass as twenty-two larger-than-life book spines tower over you at a whopping twelve feet each, providing an impressive display of must-reads.

Loganberry Books is hiding a little secret in its courtyard, proving that this bookstore has so much more to offer than the eclectic collection of books on the inside.

Larger-than-life book spines adorn the courtyard wall of Loganberry Books in the Larchmere neighborhood. The book titles, suggested by community members, offer up everything from how-to to history and everything in between. © Deb Thompson

Step inside Loganberry Books to browse an incredible selection of thousands of new, used, and antique books housed in a number of rooms of this one-story building. © Deb Thompson

LOGANBERRY BOOKS

WHAT Mural

WHERE 13015 Larchmere Blvd.

COST Free

PRO TIP Be sure to step inside for a book lover experience like no other.

The mural was installed in 2011 as part of a community art project. Over 150 book suggestions were offered up to grace the giant shelf. Twenty-two titles made the cut and include everything from knitting to self-help to romance. This massive bookshelf offers up a nice list of recommendations to start your own must-read list, and each selection is available inside.

MEMPHIS KIDDIE PARK

An amusement park for littles?

If you're looking for an amusement park with rides that are fast and furious, the Memphis Kiddie Park is not for you. Best suited for families of toddlers and preschoolers, kiddie parks appeal most to those who enjoy a slower pace and appreciate the vintage rides. Most of the rides at Memphis Kiddie Park require the riders to be under forty-eight inches tall; exceptions would be the carousel, roller coaster, and train, so if you have older children in your family, now would be a good time to leave them at home or with a sitter.

The Memphis Kiddie Park has served the community and entertained children since 1952. The Kiddie Park features ten mechanical rides, including the Little Dipper, the oldest steel kiddie coaster in continuous operation located within North America.

This unique park that beckons families to travel back to a simpler time is easily accessible from I-480 and I-71 and offers free parking and admission into the park. Visitors can purchase ride tickets and purchase food from the concession stand. Memphis Kiddie Park is the precursor to bigger things for the littles and the perfect location to begin training the tiny adventurers to become full-blown thrill seekers.

The Memphis Kiddie Park, which has survived since the 1950s, is an amusement park for families of the tiniest tots.

This amusement park for the little ones in the family features adorable vintage rides and offers family's a fun day out at an affordable price in the city. © Tonya Prater

MEMPHIS KIDDIE PARK

WHAT Amusement park

WHERE 10340 Memphis Ave., Brooklyn

COST $2.40 per ride

PRO TIP Purchase a book of twenty-five tickets to get the lowest price on rides.

55 MUSEUM OF DIVINE STATUES

What happens to the saints and angels when a church closes its doors?

Holy relics, broken angels, and faded statues have suddenly found themselves homeless as many of the Catholic churches in the area have been decommissioned. The church remains are offered to other area churches, but if the holy items cannot be placed, they often land in a church resale store. Fortunately, for some of the statues and relics, divine intervention is granted by Lou McClung, local makeup artist and art restorer.

Because makeup artistry is second nature to Lou, he quickly became very versed in taking old statues and recasting and fixing them as needed. Attaching wings, recasting arms, replacing pedestals, and ensuring that the statues are completely intact is the first step. The real magic happens in the second step when Lou resurrects the lost and forgotten statue with the strokes of his paintbrush.

The restored pieces are placed on display in the Museum of Divine Statues.

The museum is located in St. Hedwig's, an old, abandoned Catholic church that has been repurposed into a quiet,

WHAT HAPPENS WHEN YOU CROSS A MAKEUP ARTIST WITH DIVINE STATUES?

WHAT The Museum of Divine Statues

WHERE 12905 Madison Ave., Lakewood

COST $10 per person

PRO TIP Only open on Sundays, 12 p.m. to 4 p.m.

Resurrecting old Catholic statues into majestic works of art is a skill set that artist Lou McClung has mastered. Ecclesiastical statutes now reign supreme at this unique museum in a small Cleveland neighborhood. © Lou McClung

serene museum space. The museum is solely dedicated to ecclesiastical statues and sacred artifacts of the Catholic Church. Beyond the statues, there are relics, chalices, iron works, baptistery gates, and stained-glass windows. The museum is home to over two hundred pieces of restored and religious art.

Take a Sunday drive over to the Museum of Divine Statues and enjoy the restored statues by master restorer and local artist Lou McClung.

56 OH, WHAT A VIEW!

Where can you find the best views in Cleveland?

Cityscapes, Lake Erie shoreline, and fantastic bridges all encourage the viewer to sit and enjoy the view for a while. There are a few "insider" places around the city that offer better viewing opportunities than others, and we are about to spill the beans.

Top Spot #1

Bar 32, located on the 32nd floor of the Downtown Hilton Hotel, offers unobstructed views of the city skyline, Lake Erie, and the Cuyahoga River. Grab a drink and a window side table and stay awhile.

Top Spot #2

Head over to the Cleveland Clinic's main campus and find your way to the top floor of the Sydell & Arnold Miller Family Rooftop Pavilion. The floor is enclosed in glass and provides inspiring views of the city and surrounding areas.

Top Spot #3

A visit to a lakeside city wouldn't be complete without some pretty epic sunset over water photos. Of course, if you visit Edgewater Park at dusk, you can capture both the sunset over Lake Erie and a pretty nice skyline at night by simply turning around.

Top Spot #4

Merwin's Wharf is great for barge watching and bridge viewing. Sit on the patio next to the Cuyahoga River and let the world pass by.

OH, WHAT A VIEW!

The sixteen-foot Cleveland script sign in the Tremont neighborhood provides the perfect place to take a memorable photo of the Cleveland skyline, complete with water, barges, and city buildings in the backdrop.

WHAT Best Cleveland views

WHERE Various locations

COST Free

PRO TIP If possible, get out on the water for an even better skyline photo moment.

Top Spot #5

Head to the Cleveland script sign in the Tremont area and check off two must-sees on your Cleveland list in one visit. The sign has an incredible Cleveland skyline in the background, making it the perfect photo opp.

Cleveland is best known for the skyline views, but there are a few others that should be enjoyed as well.

57 OLD STONE CHURCH

What role did the Old Stone Church play in the assassination of two presidents'?

Today, the First Presbyterian Society, or Old Stone Church, which is situated in the historic heart of downtown Cleveland, may seem out of place amid the city's high-rise buildings. The hustle and bustle outside fades away as you step inside the large arched oak doors and into the beautifully ornate interior, with wooden pews, oak ceilings, and six exquisite Louis Comfort Tiffany stained-glass windows. Visitors are free to appreciate the beauty of the interior of the Romanesque church as they quiet their hearts to pray.

The oldest building to stand on Public Square and the second oldest religious organization in Cleveland, the Old Stone Church has survived two fires to stand for over 150 years. This church has seen a lot of history in its time, but no doubt one of the most memorable events was when President Abraham Lincoln's body lay in state outside while family and Clevelanders gathered inside for a memorial service. Nearly one hundred years later, the church would once again offer a memorial for a head of state following the assassination of President John F. Kennedy to a crowd of over 3,500, the largest congregation in the history of the church.

Not only is history important to the church, the arts are integral as well. The gallery features local, regional, and national artists and is often used as a meeting place for city officials. Cleveland's world-famous Holtkamp Organ Company built and installed the current organ in 1977 so the congregation and visitors can rejoice with fine choral

OLD STONE CHURCH

WHAT Religious setting

WHERE 91 Public Square

COST Free

PRO TIP Self-guided tours are available from 11 a.m. to 3 p.m., Monday through Friday.

The Old Stone Church may look out of place amid the high-rise office buildings in downtown Cleveland, but this mighty church has played an important role in Cleveland's rich history. © Deb Thompson

singing in each service. Visitors are welcome to escape the busy-ness in their everyday lives and experience the calm inside the stone walls of the church.

This property became the setting for not one but two memorial services for assassinated presidents of the United States of America.

58 OUR LADY OF LOURDES SHRINE

Do you believe in miracles?

Our Lady of Lourdes Shrine may be one of Northeast Ohio's biggest secrets. Partially obscured by a treeline on Chardon Rd., this holy complex with its park-like setting draws visitors not only from around the country but from around the world. Situated on the grounds of what used to be a vineyard, the shrine has been modeled after a similar grotto in Lourdes, France. It was there that Mary, the Blessed Mother, is said to have appeared before a young girl named Bernadette, not once but eighteen times. The on-site chapel, built in 1956, tells the story of the grotto in France through its stained-glass windows.

The hundreds of thousands of visitors who have made the pilgrimage to the sacred Euclid property since the 1920s go for the quiet tranquility and for the holy water that pours from a garden hose that runs under Mary's feet and over sacred rock chips, or relics, from the Lourdes, France, grotto.

OUR LADY OF LOURDES SHRINE

WHAT Religious setting

WHERE 21281 Chardon Rd., Euclid

COST Free

PRO TIP This may look like a park, but remember that it is a sacred religious site. Please be respectful during your visit.

A booth labeled "Testimonials of Blessings Received" is located near the grotto and displays crutches and a back brace from those who have claimed an act of physical healing after their visit.

The grotto at Our Lady of Lourdes Shrine is modeled after a grotto in Lourdes, France, where the Mother Mary is believed to have appeared to a young girl over a dozen times. © Tonya Prater

Behind the grotto at Our Lady of the Lourdes Shrine is Rosary Hill, a short uphill walkway where guests pray and meditate. There is also a Stations of the Cross on-site. © Tonya Prater

Behind the grotto are Rosary Hill and the Stations of the Cross, where visitors can walk and meditate.

Many pass by this sacred, parklike setting in Euclid every day, not knowing that it is a place where miracles occur.

135

PAINT THE TOWN

Mural, mural on the wall, who's the greatest of them all?

A cacophony of images flashes before your eyes as you pass through the Ohio City neighborhood. Paint splashed across dreary and drab city walls creates a drive-by gallery of interesting art for commuters to enjoy.

Colorful additions to the neighborhood include a full tilt video game, flying pizza, a giant leaping tiger, and Prince (a moment of silence, may he rest in peace), to name a few of the delightful scenes you'll discover. Some works are bright and colorful, while others are more sedate.

Off the main road are more murals to be discovered. Turn down side roads and alleys and the murals seemingly pop out of everywhere. Roughly a dozen murals were created when international artists descended on the city for three months to turn drab into fab.

Just a hop, skip, and a jump from the brilliant Ohio City murals is Ohio's largest mural, which stretches along the Shoreway facing Lakeview. Created by Brazilian artist Ananda Nahu, it took her roughly five weeks to complete the 620-foot-long mural that pays tribute to the area's residents.

No museum admission required when you drive the Ohio City neighborhood to see murals created by artists from around the world.

Purple rain continues to fall with this memorial tribute mural to Prince. In a fun twist, Prince is holding a partially eaten donut with sprinkles. © Deb Thompson

PAINT THE TOWN

WHAT Murals

WHERE Various locations

COST Free

PRO TIP Have someone else drive so you can enjoy the colorful displays.

60 PLAYHOUSE SQUARE OUTDOOR CHANDELIER

Where can you find the world's largest chandelier?

This is the only place in the world where 4,200 glimmering crystals can shine their light down upon you, making you the Broadway star you always wanted to be, if only for a moment. Here, reality turns to fantasy as you look up at the world's largest permanent outdoor chandelier. It is suspended forty-four feet above you, and only the truly brave stand directly under its three tons of crystals and faux gold.

Located in America's largest performing arts district outside New York's Lincoln Center, the GE Chandelier is part of a $16 million transformation process to take the beauty of the theaters into the streets of Cleveland. Its glitter and shine lures residents and visitors to the square to shop, dine, and enjoy a fabulous theater production at one of the many playhouses that line Euclid Ave.

Judging by a weekend drive down Euclid, the gamble worked. You'll find plenty of visitors enjoying the unique and historic theater district if for no other reason than to pose for a moment to take the required selfie under the dazzling chandelier, which is modeled after those found inside the theaters.

PLAYHOUSE SQUARE OUTDOOR CHANDELIER

WHAT Public art

WHERE Corner of 14th St. and Euclid Ave.

COST Free

PRO TIP Be patient if you plan to snap a photo of this attraction.

The world's largest outdoor chandelier was created as part of a $16 million renovation to enliven the streets in the historic theater district and encourage residents and visitors to explore both in and outside the theaters. © Tonya Prater

If you want to have your moment in the spotlight, head to the corner of E. 14th and Euclid Ave. Be photo ready, as this popular spot has many fans lining up to snap a picture with this giant light display.

The world's largest outdoor chandelier is located in America's largest performing arts district outside New York City's Lincoln Center and signals big things ahead for Cleveland.

61 RAISE THE CURTAIN

How did Cleveland become the second largest theater district in the United States?

In the 1920s, Playhouse Square commissioned the construction of five theaters, the Ohio, Connor Palace, State, Allen, and Hanna, which were built in under two years. Silent movies, vaudeville, and legitimate theater were all performed for the enjoyment of theater-goers. This was the entertainment hub of the time and the place to be seen.

Fast forward about forty-five years, and televisions are found in many homes and people are leaving the city by droves for suburban neighborhoods. By the late '60s only the Hanna remained open.

In the 1970s, the historic theaters were under threat of being destroyed, so the community pulled together and, one by one, restored and reopened each of the theaters. Right before the turn of the century, all the original theaters were raising their curtains.

Since then, in addition to the five original theaters, five more theaters have been added to Playhouse Square, making it second to only New York City.

From popular entertainment district with gorgeous theaters to crumbling buildings and back again, Playhouse Square is the place to see and be seen.

Five historical theaters have been completely restored and five additional theaters have been added, making Playhouse Square the second largest theater district in the United States, second only to New York City. © Deb Thompson

RAISE THE CURTAIN

WHAT Theater/Entertainment district

WHERE 1501 Euclid Ave.

COST Varies

PRO TIP Be sure to check out the world's largest outdoor chandelier in the Playhouse Square district.

More than one million guests per year walk through the doors of the theater venues in Playhouse Square. The guests descend on the square to watch more than 1,000 annual events held at ten different venues.

62 ROCK AND ROLL HALL OF FAME

Where can you see the world's largest collection of rock and roll memorabilia?

Okay, so the Rock and Roll Hall of Fame may not be a secret to anyone, but did you know it houses the world's largest collection of rock and roll memorabilia? From Johnny Cash's tour bus, to Jim Morrison's last will and testament, to Michael Jackson's iconic gold glove, there are thousands of pieces of memorabilia to enjoy on your musical walk down memory lane. The collection that encompasses six floors in the unique triangular glass building that sits along the shore of Lake Erie is straight out of a music lover's dream.

But you won't only see the iconic props, costumes, and the everyday outfits that were used by your favorite bands; your ears will be filled with songs from all genres of rock. From the crooning of the Everly Brothers, to the gospel beginnings of Elvis, to classic sounds of the Rolling Stones, to the big hair bands like Kiss and the grunge of Nirvana, music fills the halls and your ears through interactive booths and headphones.

The Rock and Roll Hall of Fame Foundation was founded in 1983 and began to induct honorees in 1986, even though the museum had no location. Cities all over the United States submitted bids for the museum that Clevelanders

---

Music is so woven into our lives that a trip to the Rock and Roll Hall of Fame is a walk down a musical memory lane.

ROCK AND ROLL HALL OF FAME

Listen to your favorite artists and see musical artifacts that include guitars, gold records, stage costumes, and even political posters and slogans inside the Rock and Roll Hall of Fame. © Tonya Prater

WHAT Museum

WHERE 1100 E. 9th St.

COST From $13.75 for youths to $23.50 for adults

PRO TIP Plan to spend a minimum of 2½ hours, even if you're not a fan of rock and roll.

sought. Cleveland had a good reason for wanting the museum to be within its city limits; after all, disc jockey Alan Freed had coined the term "rock and roll" in Cleveland in the 1950s and was integral in staging the first rock concert—the Moondog Coronation Ball—in the city. Freed was such an important figure in the history of rock and roll that his cremated remains rested within the walls of the Rock Hall until they were displaced in 2014. You can now view his uniquely shaped jukebox headstone and gravesite in none other than the prestigious Lake View Cemetery.

63 ROCKEFELLER IN CLEVELAND

How do you wish for Rockefeller wealth?

In the late 1800s the Cleveland landscape was littered with thirty oil refineries. One of these refineries was owned, in part, by none other than John D. Rockefeller. He started small and then started buying out smaller companies to add to his own. Soon thereafter Standard Oil was born. The introduction of Standard Oil skyrocketed Cleveland to the forefront of petroleum production in the United States. By 1876 Rockefeller would own 90 percent of the oil production in the country, making him the richest man alive.

To Cleveland's benefit, Rockefeller was not stingy with his profits. Schools, churches, hospitals, and social movements were often the recipients of his generosity. His financial contributions are still enjoyed today, decades after his death. He left a legacy to the city that includes the Rockefeller Park, the Cleveland Cultural Gardens, Western Reserve Historical Society, Rockefeller Park Greenhouse, the majestic Arcade, and hundreds of acres of land that are now public parks.

Although Rockefeller got his start in Cleveland, he lived the majority of his life in New York. Upon his death in 1937 he was returned to the city that jump-started his empire. Buried in Lakeview Cemetery, he rests under an obelisk, at one time the tallest monument in the state. Here visitors place dimes at his gravesite in the hopes of obtaining Rockefeller-style wealth.

A bust of Rockefeller watches over the activity at the Rockefeller Park Greenhouse in University Circle and near the Cultural Gardens. A unique attraction at the park is the Talking Garden for the Blind. © Tonya Prater

Cleveland was the recipient of much of Rockefeller's wealth, from buildings to parks to schools to social movements. Thanks to his generosity, Cleveland continues to benefit from his donations to this day. © Deb Thompson

At the turn of the twentieth century, Rockefeller was the richest man in the world. Thankfully his generous nature gave Cleveland some of its greatest attractions.

RODIN'S *THE THINKER*

What's unusual about this well-known statue?

One of the best-known works of art in the world may be Rodin's bronze sculpture of a nude man hunched over in apparent thought. Copies of the statue, appropriately dubbed *The Thinker,* can be viewed on the grounds of some of the world's most praised art museums, including the Cleveland Museum of Art located on University Circle.

It is thought that Rodin made ten of the larger-than-life sculptures during his lifetime. Upon his death in 1917, the Musée Rodin in Paris, France, was granted permission to duplicate the iconic work. Today you'll find *The Thinker* in bronze and bronze-plated plaster in over 20 locations around the globe. One even marks the grave of the creator himself.

Cleveland acquired one of the last sculptures to be made that was supervised by Rodin. This version of *The Thinker* was purchased from the artist in 1916 and generously donated to the Cleveland Museum of Art in 1917 by Cleveland resident Ralph T. King. The piece was placed in the rotunda for a short time before it was moved outdoors to be displayed, as was customary for many of Rodin's oversized works of art. Unfortunately, not all who visited the sculpture were admirers. In the wee hours of March 24, 1970, a bomb was placed on the pedestal, destroying the base and blowing off the figure's lower legs.

RODIN'S THE THINKER

WHAT Public art

WHERE 1150 East Blvd.

COST Free

PRO TIP You'll find this statue on the back terrace of the museum, overlooking Wade Park.

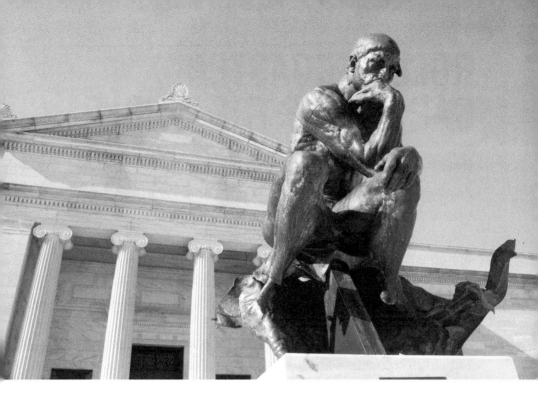

This well-known piece of art can be seen at the Cleveland Museum of Art, but you won't find it indoors with the other sculptures. This piece sits outside, overlooking Wade Lagoon. © Tonya Prater

No one was hurt in the blast, and no one was ever arrested for this act of terrorism on Cleveland's soil. It was speculated that the vandalism was the work of a radical political group in protest of the war that was going on in Vietnam. Today, the piece remains forever altered as reminder of what is wrong in our society.

The Thinker may be one of the most well recognized statues in the world, but the one in Cleveland is missing something the other versions have.

65 ROLLER COASTER CAPITAL OF THE WORLD

How loud will you scream?

Click, click, click is the only thing you hear as the roller coaster train makes its way to the top of the track and you are looking at nothing but sky. What comes next is unknown until, one stomach-churning moment later, gravity is throwing you down the other side of the track. There is nothing to do but hang on for dear life and scream at the top of your lungs as the combination of fear and fun rushes through you. This scenario is repeated on the more than fifteen coasters at the roller coaster capital of the world, Cedar Point.

Located just sixty miles west of Cleveland, this popular, adrenaline junkie destination is the premier place for roller coaster enthusiasts. Everything from the tallest, to the fastest, to the most inversions, Cedar Point offers up a coaster for everyone.

Lifelong coaster enthusiasts will appreciate that Cedar Point still operates a few of their classic coasters, like the Blue Streak, opened in 1964, the Mine Ride, Gemini, and Corkscrew.

The Top Thrill Dragster is the shortest coaster ride in the park, lasting a mere seventeen seconds but offers one of the biggest thrills as the cars are launched straight up in the air to 420 feet and hit tops speeds of 120 mph as they fly down the other side.

Take a seat on the Valravn, the tallest, fastest, and longest coaster in the park. This coaster sends riders 223 feet up in the air, dangles them over the edge, and then plunges them down the other side at a 90-degree angle. Experience multiple inversions, a 270-degree twist, as well

The Corkscrew coaster, built in 1976, is one of Cedar Point's classic steel roller coasters and, at the time, was the only coaster in the world to have three inversions. © Tonya Prater

ROLLER COASTER CAPITAL OF THE WORLD

WHAT Amusement park

WHERE 1 Cedar Point Dr., Sandusky

COST Starts at $45

PRO TIP Weekday visits tend to have fewer crowds, which equal shorter lines.

as the Immelmann maneuver. It is probably the longest 2.23-minute ride you'll ever experience.

For those who would like the thrill of a coaster without the adrenaline rush, there are coasters for you. Pick from the Mine Ride, Wilderness Run, or Woodstock Express, all of which are family-friendly coasters.

Make tracks to Sandusky, Ohio, to scream your way through some of the greatest roller coasters in the world. Hurry, though, because the coaster season is short.

SOLDIERS AND SAILORS MONUMENT

What lurks beneath the popular monument on Public Square?

The Public Square's Cuyahoga County Soldiers and Sailors Monument has stood for nearly 125 years as a tribute to the 9,000 Cuyahoga County residents who fought in the Civil War. Dedicated on July 4, 1894, the monument lists the name of each resident who served in the "War between the States," including the 1,000 who were mortally wounded and never returned home. Inside, you'll find a colorful palette with stained-glass windows, ornamental lights, Civil War artifacts, and more. Life-size bronze reliefs share some of the area's history and highlight not only President Lincoln and area financiers of the Civil War but also women who served on the Sanitary Commission. These volunteers, the equivalent of today's modern-day nurses or Red Cross workers, changed bandages, linens, and administered medication to injured soldiers.

Groupings on the outside of the monument depict the Navy, Calvary, Infantry, and Artillery, the four branches of the military that were established at that time. You'll also see a 125-foot-tall obelisk rising from the monument that depicts the Goddess of Freedom holding a shield of liberty in her hand, a representation of the freedoms we enjoy today.

While all this is visible, there is something lurking under the streets of Cleveland that few people are aware of. Is the Soldiers and Sailors Monument haunted by the very man who designed the structure, as rumors suggest? Probably not, but that doesn't stop ghost hunters and those in search of a thrill from visiting each year around Halloween

PUBLIC SQUARE'S CUYAHOGA COUNTY SOLDIERS AND SAILORS MONUMENT

WHAT Public monument

WHERE 3 Public Square

COST Free

PRO TIP Keep an eye on the News and Events section of www.soldiersandsailors.com to see when the next tunnel tour is offered.

Many Clevelanders drive past this impressive memorial and marvel at the detail and craftsmanship of architect and sculptor Levi Scofield without knowing that the monument is open for free tours. © Deb Thompson

to explore the tunnels under the monument on Public Square. The dark, damp, and narrow catacombs seem to be the perfect environment for a hair-raising experience, but in reality, the system of circular tunnels was built to support the weight of the shrine and nothing more. Or was it?

Some claim the popular monument in Cleveland's Public Square, constructed to honor those who fought in the Civil War, is haunted.

67 SOPLATA WARPLANE GRAVEYARD

Have you ever seen a graveyard full of warplanes?

Obsessions come in many shapes and sizes, and in Walter Soplata's case, his hoarding fixation started with planes. Despite having very little money as an adult and in most regards, living a very frugal life, Walter's fascination with warplanes fueled an obsession that led to the purchase of many planes in his lifetime.

While many of the planes appear to be rusting away as permanent fixtures on a plot of land that Walter purchased to house them, several planes have been sold, restored, and are now airworthy once more.

SOPLATA WARPLANE GRAVEYARD

WHAT Warplanes

WHERE Newbury

COST Free

PRO TIP This collection is located on private property and not open to the public.

As a child growing up during the recession, Walter dreamed of aircraft and sought a job in the military. This was short-lived as he was discharged from the armed forces due to a stutter. That didn't stop him from working around planes. He later found a job working at a scrapyard during and after World War II where he helped to move thousands of engines off warplanes that were considered surplus. He was able to purchase dozens of planes at scrap prices. Most planes only cost him a few hundred dollars, but after he purchased them, he had to find ingenious ways to transport them to the piece of property he owned in Newbury, which is east of Cleveland.

Soplata's Warplane Graveyard was one man's mission to preserve many of the planes that have been used in battle by the United States during WWII, resulting in a collection of planes that at one time may have rivaled many museum collections. © Tonya Prater

Some of the WWII-era planes in Walter's collection include a B-25, BT-15, a Goodyear FG-ID, a wrecked B-57 Canberra bomber, and a FG-1D Corsair. At one point, the warplane graveyard was open to visitors and drew up to thirty people a day, but tours stopped years before Walter's death as his health began to fail. His family has kept what remained of Walter Soplata's his collection intact as he requested.

One man's fascination with planes leads to a one-of-a-kind graveyard of WWII warplanes that few are lucky enough to see.

68

SPEND THE NIGHT WITH FRANK

Do you love architecture?

During the height of his career, Frank Lloyd Wright continued to design and build residential homes. Only one hundred were constructed, which he dubbed "Usonians" and represent the best of his work. The Louis Penfield House, a twenty-minute drive from Downtown Cleveland, is one such house.

In true Frank Lloyd Wright style, he used materials that were readily available to construct the home. He used his master skills as an architect to leave the integrity of the landscape as natural as possible while providing the best views.

The Louis Penfield House stands out as a unique building in the Wright portfolio. Built for Mr. Penfield, who was a tall drink of water at 6'8", Mr. Wright's signature styling of small entryways and narrow passages had to be switched up to accommodate Mr. Penfield's size. At the Penfield House you'll find taller ceilings, slim ribbon windows, and tall yet narrow doorways.

There are only a handful of places in the United States that afford you the opportunity to stay in a Frank Lloyd house; the Penfield House in Willoughby Hills is one of them.

SPEND THE NIGHT WITH FRANK

Not too far outside of Cleveland awaits a very special experience for fans of Frank Lloyd Wright. This one-of-a-kind home can be reserved for nightly stays for guests to experience and explore Frank's architecture, with no supervision or slippers required. © PenfieldHouse

WHAT Architecture

WHERE 2203 River Rd., Willoughby Hills

COST $275 per night

PRO TIP House is for sale if you'd like to own a piece of history for $1.7 million.

All this can be experience firsthand at this living architecture home. Tours are not available, but those who love Frank Lloyd Wright's work have the opportunity to fully enjoy his craftsmanship by living in the house for one night or many. Immerse yourself inside his home. Nothing is off limits, no slippers required. Touch, feel, and breathe the work of a master architect during your stay.

69

SQUIRE'S CASTLE

What happened to the castle?

Grand plans to build a mansion with a gatekeeper's cottage was on the mind of Feargus B. Squire, an executive with the Standard Oil Company, in 1890. Plans were sketched out to build two residences in English-German baronial hall style. They would be constructed on the 525 acres owned by Mr. Squire in the Chagrin Valley.

Digging silt stone from a nearby quarry the construction workers started on the gatekeeper's cottage first. Setting the stones, one by one, the workers created an elaborate design that included parapets, turrets, and towers. Soon the cottage took on the look of a miniature-sized castle.

Mr. Squire may have not have had a complete stamp of approval from the Missus, however, on the new living arrangements. History tells that she was not one for spending time in the country and may be the main reason construction on the country estate never began. Instead, Mr. Squire used the gatekeeper's cottage for many years as a weekend retreat before selling the home and land in the early 1920s, which was eventually purchased by Cleveland Metroparks in 1925.

Long left to the elements and vandals today, what remains is more ruin than home, with only the walls and

SQUIRE'S CASTLE

WHAT Building

WHERE North Chagrin Nature Center, River Rd., Willoughby Hills

COST Free

PRO TIP Pack a picnic and enjoy the castle as a backdrop to your family picnic.

Built in 1890 the castle was intended to be a gatekeeper's cottage for the country estate that Feargus B. Squire intended to build. However, the estate was never built, and Mr. Squire used the cottage for his country escapes until he sold the property in the 1920s. © Tonya Prater

turret standing. The basement has been filled in and interior walls removed, but visitors are still welcome to wander through this once magnificent home.

A mini castle built in the late 1800s still stands today and is open for visitors to walk through the crumbling ruins.

70 STAR LIGHT, STAR BRIGHT

What do you see tonight?

High up on a gentle rise of land in East Cleveland sits a concrete and steel observatory finished in red brick with stone trimmings. Its heyday long past and now left to the ravages of time, the Warner and Swasey Observatory was once an important scientific landmark on the neighborhood's landscape.

Used to gaze upon the heavens above, first with a 9.5-inch refractor telescope and later, around 1940, with a 24-inch Burrell Schmidt telescope, the stars were studied and important scientific discoveries made. After the new telescope arrived, it was used to prove the theory that the Milky Way was a spiral galaxy and that red giant stars resided in the center of it.

Due to the growth of Cleveland and the ever-growing light pollution, the Burrell Schmidt telescope was moved from the Warner and Swasey Observatory to a new location thirty miles farther east. In its stead, a 36-inch telescope replaced the Burrell Schmidt, and the observatory opened to the public. It became known as one of the best public astronomical viewing locations in the country. It continued

---

A once important landmark in Cleveland, the Warner and Swasey Observatory now sits empty off a small rise east of the city.

The observatory, a once prominent addition to the city of Cleveland, has been left to the elements, nature, and graffiti artists. Ivy climbs the walls while spray paint art adorns the brick and the walls within. © Deb Thompson

STAR LIGHT, STAR BRIGHT

WHAT Abandoned building

WHERE 1975 Taylor Rd., East Cleveland

COST Free

PRO TIP The observatory is on private property and should not be entered without permission from the owner.

to be enjoyed by visitors for twenty years before being permanently closed in 1980.

Today, the observatory sits empty on that same overlook, a reminder of how this East Cleveland neighborhood once had dark enough skies to view the heavens above.

71 STREET ART

What makes your commute more enjoyable?

Every day thousands of commuters use Euclid Ave., a main thoroughfare, to connect them from Downtown through Playhouse Square, past Cleveland State University, and into University Circle. This six-and-half-mile stretch of road, one of the city's most historic, could be a rather staid commute of boring pavement and brake lights. Instead, with the help of artisans and landscapers, the Euclid Corridor Transportation Project (ECTP) was born.

The ECTP was started to create a more appealing visual view and to make everyday amenities more enjoyable. Artists used their creative skills to craft artistically inspired benches, guideposts, crosswalks, sidewalk art, and trash receptacles. Of course, the art helps make the commute a bit more enjoyable, but those walking may receive the biggest benefit, as they are able to view the art up close and personal.

In addition to turning the mundane into less of an eye strain, three street sculptures were strategically placed along the route. In University Circle, you'll find Osmosis, a sandstone-colored, cairn shaped sculpture that rises in the median between traffic lanes. Chorus Line Luminaries dance along in Playhouse Square, near the East 14th St. RTA station; and in East Cleveland, at the end of the ECTP, is an Interactive Poetry Project made up of spheres and planks.

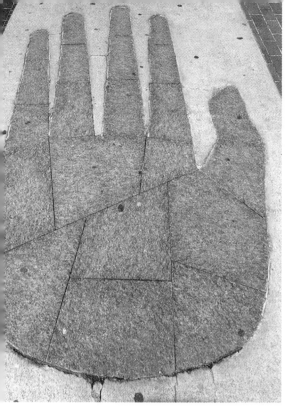

Located on the sidewalk that runs parallel to westbound traffic on Euclid Ave., the piece of sidewalk art greets pedestrians rushing past. Hopefully some take a moment to glance down to enjoy this playful installation. © Deb Thompson

STREET ART

WHAT Art

WHERE Euclid Ave. from Downtown to East Cleveland

COST Free

PRO TIP Stretch your legs a bit by parking and walking part of this stretch to fully enjoy the works of art.

Art can be found almost everywhere in this artistic-centric city, including on the daily commute to and from work.

72

TAKE A BITE OUT OF CLEVELAND

What foods is Cleveland famous for?

Philadelphia has cheesesteak, Chicago has pizza, Detroit has Coney dogs, and NYC has cheesecake. Almost every major city in America has a food that is considered their claim to fame. In Cleveland, however, it's hard to claim just one; instead, they claim three. The Polish Boy, Slyman's Corned Beef Sandwich, and Pierogies seem to be the top contenders for Cleveland's most famous bites.

The Polish Boy has been a messy city favorite since the 1940s and consists of a kielbasa link on a bun, which is then covered with a layer of French fries, heavily drizzled with barbecue sauce, and then topped off with coleslaw. The history is vague on the origin of this oddly layered sandwich, but it has been on restaurant menus for more than seventy years.

Another claim to fame food is the famous Slyman's Deli Corned Beef Sandwich. Slyman's has been piling up five inches of corned beef on bread to the delight of its customers for over fifty years. Proof that this sandwich continues to be a city favorite can be found in the lines that go out the door on a daily basis.

Cleveland has many foodie options, but there are three this city can claim as their signature dish.

Slyman's is famous for their piled high corned beef sandwiches. Five inches of corned beef is stacked between slices of rye bread and served up six days a week. This famous sandwich is enough to feed two people. © Deb Thompson

TAKE A BITE OUT OF CLEVELAND

WHAT Food

WHERE Various locations

COST Varies

PRO TIP Visit the Westside Market to try many of these bites at one stop.

Pierogies, those delicious moon shaped potato dumplings, were introduced by European settlers to the area in the early twentieth century. They are so popular that they are found in many area restaurants. So famous, they even have their own festival each summer.

73

TAKE A HIKE

What can you find along this historic mule route?

Walk or pedal the eighty-five mile historic trail where mules used to pull canal boats filled with people and things along the Ohio & Erie Canal. The mules have long since disappeared, but the towpath trail where hooves pulled thousands of loads remains and today is used by more than two million people annually.

Within the city, the towpath can be found along Scranton Rd. in the Flats district where the canal meets the Cuyahoga River. Only a short ⅔ mile along the river, it takes visitors to a pier overlooking the river for an up-close view of container ships from around the globe.

Not too far away, in the Cleveland Metroparks at Harvard Rd., just east of Jennings, is as far north as you'll go on the trail. Here is where you can start an eighty-four-mile journey south. This portion of the trail takes you into the Cuyahoga Valley National Park. While traversing this eight-mile trail, you'll cross two cable-style bridges that span Warner and Granger roads.

Once you enter the Cuyahoga Valley National Park, you get into the heart of the towpath. Discover a lock from 1905 that has been fully restored, enjoy the beauty of Pinery Narrows, a stunning, 2.7-mile stretch of trail,

Grab your fat tire bike or hiking shoes and head out to explore over eighty miles of trails along the Ohio & Erie Canal.

Back in the day mules pulled cargo-laden boats through the Ohio & Erie Canal. Today, those grooves created by mule hooves long ago provide the perfect pathway for hiking and biking. © Tonya Prater

TAKE A HIKE

WHAT Nature trails

WHERE Various locations

COST Free

PRO TIP Be sure to swing by the Canal Exploration Center at Lock 3 to explore the thousands of years of history of the region.

explore historic homes and settlements, find a stunning waterfall, and stop at a local favorite, Beaver Marsh.

Those not keen on experiencing the path via foot or wheel can hop aboard a train on the Cuyahoga Valley Scenic Railroad or experience the path from the water on the *St. Helena III*, a working replica of a canal-era freight barge.

74

THAT'S A WRAP!

What's a city to do when plagued with unsightly utility boxes?

Art is popping up all over Cleveland. Recent art installations have fixated on the drab traffic control boxes and utility boxes that can be seen along the city streets to offer pops of color and brighten communities. The colorful art boxes, or art murals as they're called, serve another purpose as well. They deter vandals from painting the boxes with graffiti. Plus, each wrap is made of durable, adhesive film similar to the wraps you see on vehicles, which will help protect the boxes from damage caused by inclement weather.

Installations can be found throughout University Circle along Euclid Ave. between E. 105th and E. 123rd and also in the heart of Downtown Cleveland, between Public Square and Playhouse Square. Though they are both similar in execution, they are the brainchild of different organizations.

The University Circle art boxes were created by eight illustration majors from the Cleveland Institute of Art. The students were tasked with the responsibility to create a series of scenes from Cleveland and University Circle from the four-decade span of the 1920s to 1960s. The Art Box Project is part of UCI's Euclid Gateway Vision campaign and

---

Colorful art boxes that camouflage traffic and utility boxes in the city can be found in two of Cleveland's most artistic districts.

Kasey Olson

Located in both downtown and the University Circle areas are utility boxes wrapped to look like pieces of art that brighten the landscape and many Clevelanders' commutes. © Deb Thompson
    The boxes are wrapped with a special film to protect the boxes from damage from the natural elements as well as would be vandals who like to leave their own mark. © Deb Thompson

was implemented in cooperation with the City of Cleveland and Greater Cleveland Regional Transit Authority.

The Connections that Matter Art Box Mural Series, or Crown Castle Art Box Collection, is a project of Downtown Cleveland Alliance and its City Advocates Program—in partnership with Crown Castle. This installation features nine utility boxes that have been wrapped in vinyl reproductions of winning artwork submitted by area artists.

Next time you're out in the city, take a few minutes to seek out these fun pieces of art.

75 THE POLITICIAN: A TOY

Does art have to be pretty to make a statement?

No one has ever said art needs to be pretty, and *The Politician: A Toy* is a prime example. The sculpture that stands on the lawn of Cleveland State University near the corner of 18th St. and Chester Ave. may be colorful with its bright primary colors, but appealing to the eye it is not. Even a former Mayor of Cleveland, Michael White, was reported to have opposed the piece because it was not aesthetically pleasing.

While it may lack beauty, unlike some art pieces this large installment does get its point across loud and clear. This statue was created by Billie Lawless, a politically charged artist from Buffalo, New York. The piece, funded by private donations, weighs in at more than twenty tons and stands over forty feet tall. It's enclosed in a wrought iron fence that depicts political promises made by a previous president that never came to fruition.

The wheels are a turnin' on this sculpture, which is in motion day and night, but surprisingly it doesn't seem to

---

THE POLITICIAN: A TOY

WHAT Public art

WHERE Corner of 18th St. and Chester Ave.

COST Free

PRO TIP This is only one of the public art displays you'll find on the CSU campus; allow time to explore the others.

Designed by politically charged artist Billie Lawless, his work The Politician: A Toy, *an outdoor sculpture, proves that you don't have to be pretty to be eye-catching or to make a statement.* © Deb Thompson

get anywhere as its mouth spews promises unfulfilled to the hundreds of CSU students who pass by daily. Maybe they, too, think the statue could be prettied up a bit. Students did go as far as discussing the possibility of making a community garden around the sculpture, which the artist abhorred. His response? If he thought a garden would enhance his artwork, he would have planted one himself.

Beauty truly is in the eye of the beholder or, in this case, the artist. This edgy sculpture is unlike many others found around the city.

76

THEY HAVE LANDED

What is hidden within?

Along a busy street, a large orb sits quietly on the earth while two nearby partial orbs appear to be pushing their way out of the ground, or perhaps they have crashed landed here from a place far, far away. The truth, unfortunately, isn't quite as entertaining, although the previous ideas help keep the art shrouded in a bit of mystery.

Created by local artist Loren Naji, the sculpture was intended to look out of place within the surroundings. And it does. The full plywood sphere comes in at an impressive eight feet in diameter and weighs in at 3,000 pounds and

is hollow inside. The sculptures "allude to the sphere, our universal form as well as planets, spaceships and alien life that just landed," said Naji.

If you take a few minutes to stop and take a closer look at the orbs, you'll find that they are so much more than a public art installation. For within the largest orb are secrets of years gone by—it is the keeper of the time capsule that was sealed inside in 2011. One can only imagine what items made its way inside. Is there a family photo? Perhaps a gaming system or CD? Maybe a copy of that day's newspaper? It will all remain hidden until the opening of the capsule on September 23, 2050, thirty-nine years after it was sealed.

THEY HAVE LANDED

A massive orb sits outside a Rapid Transit Station in the Ohio City neighborhood. Part art, part time capsule, the wooden work of art is set to be opened in 2050.

A bronze marker placed on the ground in front of the They Have Landed sculpture tells the story of the art installed by Loren Naji, a local artist, in September 2011.

WHAT Public art

WHERE 2350 Lorain Ave.

COST Free

PRO TIP Street parking near Westside Market

Located on a busy throughway,
but often overlooked by passersby,
this piece of public art is much more
than it seems at first glance.

77

TINY LIBRARY PATRONS

Can you find all the tiny patrons?

Scamper around the Eastman Reading Garden located at the downtown public library and you are sure to stumble across some of the most adorable library patrons. Small in stature, bronze in color, these playful, cartoonish sculptures are engaged in fun activities like reading, climbing, acting like acrobats, or carrying letters and symbols.

Enter the garden, off Rockwell Ave., through a bronze gate and keep your eyes open for these playful characters. Peek down at the gate foundation to see two figures greeting you as you start to walk into the garden. Stop at the gate and look for all the other frolicsome characters.

There are four dancing along the top of the gate and another sitting on the gate door and another hanging from the center of the gate. Once you walk into the garden, be sure to look for more mischievous friends on benches, window sills, and in the gardens. Find them together or alone as they entertain the garden visitors.

The tiny library patrons, installed at the library in 1998, are from the creative genius of Tom Otterness, considered to be one of the world's best public sculptors. Since then, a countless number of library visitors have found joy in discovering these whimsical works of art.

TINY LIBRARY PATRONS

WHAT Sculptures

WHERE 325 Superior Ave. E.

COST Free

PRO TIP For fun, be sure to find the tiny patron holding the dollar sign.

*The immense bronze gate guards adorned with tiny patrons guards entry
to the Eastman Reading Garden beyond. The garden connects the original
library with a new addition and provides an oasis in the middle of the city to
read your favorite book. © Deb Thompson*

*The tiny letter-stealing patron is hanging out on the bronze gate that leads
into the Reading Garden at Cleveland Public Library. The tiny sculpture is
joined by a group of friends who live throughout the garden and brings a
smile to all who visit. © Deb Thompson*

Enjoy frolicking figures while relaxing
in the Cleveland Public Library
Eastman Reading Garden, an oasis
in the middle of the city.

78 TIPTOE THROUGH THE TREETOPS

What can you see from above?

There is no need to brush off the passport and buy an expensive ticket to an exotic locale to walk suspended above the trees. Treetop adventures happen right here at the Judith and Maynard H. Murch IV Canopy Walk and Kalberer Family Emergent Tower at Holden Arboretum.

The fun begins as soon as you enter the park and smell the blooming of flowers lining the path between the visitors center and the start of the canopy walk six-tenths of a mile away. Arriving at the canopy walk, you'll start your adventure on a wooden boardwalk ramp that takes you to twenty-four feet above the earth. From there the real adventure begins as the boardwalk ends and the grated hanging bridges, suspended in the treetops, begins.

The three bridges form a V shape and start on the edge of a ravine. As you start your walk the ground starts to fall farther and farther away until you are standing sixty-five feet above the forest floor. The walk takes you through the trees where you are suddenly eye to eye with creatures you once looked up at. As you walk the bridges, gaze around and below for a whole new perspective of the forest as you

---

Take the path that gently leads toward the treetops to gain an entirely new perspective of life amongst the branches and the forest floor below.

WALK THROUGH THE TREETOPS

WHAT Hike

WHERE 9550 Sperry Rd., Kirtland

COST $14

PRO TIP This attraction is seasonal: April 1 through November 1.

Get a bird's-eye view of the forest floor below without having to soar like an eagle. Holden Arboretum takes you on a journey through the trees and up above the treetops with the Canopy Walk and Emergent Tower. © Deb Thompson

watch critters scamper about and view birds resting on branches. It's a whole new world when you are in the trees instead of below them.

When you are ready for a bird's-eye view of the forest, make tracks to the Kalberer Family Emergent Tower, which takes you up 120 feet' and offers a 360-degree view of the surrounding area. Feel the wind on your face as you see how nature and people connect. On clear days visitors can see all the way to Lake Erie.

79

TOYNBEE TILE

What hidden meaning do these tiles hold?

TOYNBEE IDEA IN MOVIE 2001

RESURRECT DEAD ON PLANET JUPITER

I'M ONLY ONE MAN AND WHEN I CAUGHT A FATAL DISEASE.

THEY GLOATED OVER ITS DEATH.

THAT'S WHEN I BEGGED THEM NOT TO DESTROY IT.

THANK YOU AND GOODBYE.

Tiles embedded with these words or similar have been appearing on streets across the United States, mostly along the mid-Atlantic coast, since the mid-1980s. In a weird twist, the tiles were pressed into roads without notice or permission and continued to show up until the early 2000s.

Over the years several hundred tiles have been discovered, but they often fall victim to repaving and road maintenance, thus becoming lost to history forever.

Little is known about how the tiles began, but it is believed they were originated by a Philadelphia artist and were the result of his campaign to resurrect life on Jupiter,

---

A call to resurrect life on planet Jupiter is being advertised on streets across the United States.

Little is known about the Toynbee Tiles, pleas to resurrect life on Jupiter, that have turned up in mid-Atlantic and midwestern cities. This tile is one of a kind due to its size. © Deb Thompson

TOYNBEE TILE

WHAT Art installation

WHERE West Third and Prospect

COST Free

PRO TIP Use the toynbeeidea. com site to find more tile locations across the United States.

an idea the artist concocted by combining part of an autobiography, *Experiences,* and the movie *2001: A Space Odyssey*.

At one point three of these tiles were located in Cleveland. Two were destroyed due to road construction, and the only one that remains is the one at West Third and Prospect. This tile is larger than most, coming in at around 24 inches by 12 inches, with nonfaded words. Why three were placed in Cleveland remains a mystery.

80

UNDERGROUND RAILROAD

How many slaves escaped the South through Cleveland's Underground Railroad network?

It's impossible to ever know how many slaves fleeing the South escaped to freedom in the North using the Underground Railroad. Most experts place the number somewhere around 100,000, which, surprisingly, is a small percentage of the slaves held captive during that time. During the 1860s there were almost 4 million slaves in the South, which means that less than 3 percent successfully escaped suffering and oppression.

The Underground Railroad system was spread throughout the Midwest and Summit, Medina and Cuyahoga counties helped 3,500 of the 100,000 slaves gain freedom. Of those 3,500, one Hinckley man, Hiram Miller, helped 1,000 of them escape north to Canada through the ingenious method of shipping the runaway slaves in dry goods boxes. Upon arrival in Canada, slaves immediately had the freedom they so desperately sought.

A marker noting Hiram Miller's significant contribution to the Underground Railroad was located on property at W. 130th St. north of Laurel Rd. in Hinckley for over sixty-five years. However, as time is wont to do, the landscape changed, the house and barn were cleared from the land, and nothing remained of

UNDERGROUND RAILROAD

WHAT Historical significance

WHERE Hinckley

COST Free

PRO TIP The historical marker noting Hiram Miller's work is on display at the Brunswick Historical Society.

A historic marker, that now resides at the Brunswick Historical Society, tells the brief story of Hiram Miller an individual that worked tirelessly to help slaves escape the south. He shipped slaves to Canada in dry good boxes helping approximately 1,000 find freedom. © Brunswick Area Historical Society

Hiram Miller's work except the standing historical marker. Due to the land no longer having anything significant to represent him, the marker was removed and donated to the Brunswick Historical Society, where it remains today.

One local man helped a thousand slaves escape to freedom through the Underground Railroad system.

81 UNIVERSITY CIRCLE

Where can you find the world's largest concentration of art and culture in one mile?

University Circle packs more arts and culture into one square mile than anywhere else in the world, including New York and Paris. Four miles from downtown, the area is home to three hospitals and colleges and over a dozen museums, some established over one hundred years ago. This is one area of Cleveland that should be on everyone's bucket list.

The Cleveland Museum of Art is one of the nation's top museums due to its exquisite collection of masterpieces that range from ancient Egypt to modern times. Thanks to the generosity of well-known industrialists of the nineteenth century, the extensive permanent collection has always been free to explore.

Severance Hall has been home to the Cleveland Orchestra, the third most recorded orchestra in the world, since 1931. The hall, an architectural marvel built during the Great Depression, possesses one of the finest examples of Art Deco décor in the United States. It is also home to the Norton Memorial Organ that features over 6,000 pipes ranging from 32 feet to 7 inches in length.

The Cleveland Museum of Natural History contains more than four million specimens, including the largest collection of documented human skeletons in the world, the most utilized museum collection on the planet.

University Circle is known throughout the world for its high concentration of arts and culture within one single square mile.

The area called University Circle encompasses one square mile of medical, educational, and cultural institutions and attractions that are considered to be some of the best in their class in the world. © Tonya Prater

Celebrating 150 years, the Western Reserve Historical Society is the oldest cultural institution in University Circle. Three museums in one, this complex includes the Cleveland History Center, the Crawford Auto Aviation Museum, and a research library.

It may not be classified as a museum, but Glidden House may be the perfect spot to rest after a full day of exploration. The only boutique hotel within University Circle, this mansion belonged to the Glidden Paint moguls and features an impressive art collection of its own to complement the historic suites and modern hotel-style rooms.

82 VERMILION GORE ORPHANAGE

Do long-ago children still haunt this land?

The wind quietly whispers through the trees while nature's residents are eerily silent. No birds singing or squirrels running about the crumbling foundation of a long-ago orphanage.

There is no shortage of ghost stories surrounding the Vermilion Gore Orphanage that used to inhabit these lands. But one story stands out among the rest, and that particular story goes a little like this...

A couple from Indiana, who loved being parents, lost their children, most likely to one of the many plagues of that era. To ease their heartache, they decided to start an orphanage. In 1903, they opened a home for wayward children, but sadly, as is ought to happen, the orphanage faced financial issues, and it closed its doors in 1916. History doesn't tell what happened to the lost souls of the children who now found themselves homeless again.

Sometime after the orphanage closed, another began in the same spot and went by the name Gore Orphanage. As disturbing as the name sounds, it's important to note that the term *gore* refers to the wedge shape of land the home sat on and, at the time, didn't have a nefarious meaning.

Indulge in one of Ohio's most famous ghost stories, which may still haunt the land today.

The home of one of Ohio's most famous ghost stories, the Vermilion Gore Orphanage burned to the ground in the early twentieth century, and all that remains today is a stone pillar. © Library of Congress http://www.loc.gov/pictures/item/oh0185.photos.126601p/

VERMILION GORE ORPHANAGE

WHAT Haunting

WHERE 8365 Gore Orphanage Rd., Vermilion

COST Free

PRO TIP Visit the nearby Cry Baby Bridge

One night, under mysterious circumstances, the home burnt to the ground. Legend says that Old Man Gore, the orphanage owner, started the fire. The fire quickly engulfed the home and burnt it to the ground, the young occupants, unable to escape the fierce blaze, perished.

The townspeople, wanting to brush away their tragic history, simply knocked down what remained of the home and let nature reclaim the land. Soon after, whispers of ghostly children playing in the woods late at night or begging for someone to help them started to spread and has remained as one of Ohio's most famous ghost stories.

83

VISIT ALICE IN WONDERLAND

Who fell down the rabbit hole?

Over the course of forty-six years, millionaire Andrew Carnegie donated money to build more than 2,500 libraries across the United States. Fourteen of those libraries were built throughout Cleveland during the iron, steel, and oil industry boom. Today, six continue to operate as libraries, including the largest Cleveland Public Library branch, Carnegie West.

Wander through this library until you stumble across the playful Alice in Wonderland tiles dancing across the face of the ornately decorated fireplace. Grab a book, preferably *Alice in Wonderland,* sink deeply into a nearby chair, and get lost in a world that exists only down the rabbit hole.

The eight Alice in Wonderland Grueby Art Pottery tiles above the fireplace invite those of all ages to slip into another world, if only for a little while. The artist, William Grueby, designed fourteen six-inch Alice in Wonderland tiles especially for a 1908 exhibit at the Chicago Art

---

Beyond books, the Carnegie West Library is home to one-of-a-kind Grueby Art Pottery tiles inspired by Alice in Wonderland.

Playful characters from Alice in Wonderland *are designed on Grueby tiles and dance along the top of the fireplace in the children's section at the Carnegie West Library in the Ohio City neighborhood.* © Deb Thompson

Institute. His work is easily identified by his signature trademark of using a matte green glaze on the pottery, which is showcased in the background of these unique tiles.

What happened to the remaining six tiles from the original collection remains a mystery. much like the mystery of how Alice fell down the rabbit hole.

84

VISIT THE FOUR CONTINENTS

Are you ready for a trip around the world?

In the early 1920s, when Playhouse Square was becoming Cleveland's theater district, it was decided that the theater marquee should be on Euclid Ave.; therefore the stage was built at the back of the long lot. At the time, this meant that the State Theater had the world's longest theater lobby.

VISIT THE FOUR CONTINENTS

WHAT Murals

WHERE 1519 Euclid Ave.

COST Free

PRO TIP Enjoy the murals on the way to your seat for a Broadway show.

What wasn't as well-known was that within the lobby the walls were adorned with four murals created by American modernist James Daugherty. The lobby, at 320 feet long gave Mr. Daugherty plenty of empty canvas to create incredible works of art. Not deterred by the massive job ahead, he decided to focus on theatrical scenes from the four continents of the globe. Creating four fifty-foot murals, he painted *The Spirit of Pageantry—Africa, The Spirit of Drama—Europe, The Spirit of Cinema—America,* and *The Spirit of Fantasy—Asia.* The art was so impressive that *The Spirit of Cinema—America* was on the February 1970 *Life* magazine cover.

For almost fifty years theater-goers enjoyed the colorful murals as they made the stroll from the front of the lobby to their seats. The doors of the State Theater were shuttered in 1969 and remained closed until it

The elaborate, jaw-dropping interior of the State Theater in the Playhouse Square district has its walls adorned with four massive murals by American Modernist James Daugherty.The murals depict theatrical scenes from around the world. © Ken Blaze, shared courtesy of Playhouse Square

underwent a restoration project from 1979 to 1984, when it was reopened for traveling Broadway performances. Surprisingly, the murals survived their years on the lobby walls and can now be enjoyed by those going to the theater today.

Travel the four continents, from America to Europe to Africa and Asia, without ever having to board a plane; simply visit the State Theater.

85 WALL OF WHALES

Is it possible to spot a pod of whales in Cleveland?

One may expect to see seagulls or Canada geese along the Lake Erie water line in Cleveland. You may even expect to catch a glimpse of the Lake Erie Monster, if such a creature really does exist, but you don't expect to see whales. Yet that is what daily morning commuters may see if they keep their eyes open on their morning drive into the city. A pod of humpback whales can be seen swimming in a sea of blue along busy I-90.

At first glance, you may think your weary eyes are playing tricks on you, but you'll quickly realize these gentle giants are part of a mural painted by world-famous artist and environmentalist Robert Wyland to raise awareness of the importance of caring for the world's oceans. This mural isn't simply fun to look at; it was painted with purpose—to increase the knowledge that all the earth's aquatic systems are connected.

Robert Wyland has painted a total of one hundred whaling walls and aquatic paintings around the world over the course of the past twenty-seven years. Twenty-four of those paintings are now extinct, but his seventy-fifth painting, *Song of the Whales,* which took a record six days to paint on the exterior of the metal-paneled Cleveland

---

The gentle giants that swim along the shore of Lake Erie aren't there simply for decoration but to raise awareness about a crisis affecting our environment.

The Wall of Whales mural wasn't painted simply to brighten the exterior walls of the Cleveland Public Power Plant but to raise awareness of environmental hazards that threaten our oceans.
© *Tonya Prater*

THE WALL OF WHALES MURAL

WHAT Mural

WHERE 5251 North Marginal Rd.

COST Free

PRO TIP This is one of dozens of murals you'll find around Cleveland. Spend a day exploring the murals in Ohio City and Collinwood.

Public Power Plant, has remained since its dedication on October 6, 1997, despite receiving damage from Hurricane Sandy.

So forget the expensive whale watching cruise next time you're on vacation. Instead grab your camera and head down North Marginal Rd. where you're guaranteed to get a great photo of a whale family in motion. No need for binoculars or special camera equipment to capture this colossal masterpiece.

86 WESTWARD HO!

What is Cleveland's oldest building?

In the early nineteenth century, if you wanted to travel from one city to the next, it wasn't as simple as jumping in a car or catching the next flight out of town. Instead, you would arrange for a seat on a stagecoach—a horse-drawn transportation carriage. Once you boarded the carriage, you would, as a rule, squeeze in tight with up to a dozen other passengers. Stagecoach stops along well-worn routes allowed passengers to stretch, grab a bite to eat, or even spend the night. These were spaced fifteen to twenty miles apart, where horses would be changed out before a new galloping team would continue the arduous journey.

WESTWARD HO!

WHAT Dunham Tavern Museum

WHERE 6709 Euclid Ave., Cleveland

COST $5 per person

PRO TIP Takes less than an hour to complete the tour.

In 1819, a young East Coast couple built a house in northern Ohio and started to farm the land. A few years after they began their farming venture, the Buffalo-Cleveland-Detroit post road cut a path near their homestead. With an entrepreneurial spirit, and not wanting to let the opportunity pass them by, the couple converted part of their home to a tavern and became a stagecoach stop, offering refreshments to travelers; thus the Dunham Tavern was born. This establishment thrived on the prairie as a social and political hub.

After the railroad became the main mode of transportation, stagecoach stops faded from existence, but the Dunham Tavern, the oldest building in Cleveland,

When stagecoaches were the main means of transportation across the country, stagecoach stops were a must for changing out horses, stretching your legs, enjoying some refreshments, and exchanging social and political information. The Dunham Tavern is one such stop and is the oldest building in Cleveland. © Deb Thompson

A bronze historic marker sits outside the Dunham Tavern house, dating back to 1824, identifying it as the oldest building in Cleveland still standing in its original location. The building was dedicated as a museum in 1936. © Deb Thompson

remains today in its original spot. It is tucked in between industrial buildings and sandwiched between busy roads, but the building-turned-museum continues to welcome guests and share the history of Ohio's original settlers.

Stagecoaches may no longer stop at this establishment, but its history remains within its walls and welcomes visitors to explore the past.

87

WHERE THE FISHES SWIM

What lives in the smokestacks?

What happens when you build a powerhouse just to power electric streetcars and then streetcars go the way of the horse and buggy? Well, if you are FirstEnergy Powerhouse, you repurpose the building to become an entertainment complex and when you still have thousands of empty square feet, you toss an aquarium into the mix.

FirstEnergy Powerhouse, located on the west bank of the Cuyahoga River, is best known for its tall smokestacks and arched windows. It was built in 1892 in the Romanesque revival style and its design resembled that of the European factories of the time. The powerhouse was the first plant strictly dedicated to powering Cleveland's streetcars. In 1901, the powerhouse doubled in size to meet the demands of more streetcars, but a few years later the business shuttered its operation in 1920 due to the growing popularity of the automobile.

The Greater Cleveland Aquarium opened to the public in 2012. Marinescape NZ Limited, a New Zealand company, had the goal of using as much of the original powerhouse in the design of the aquarium as possible. Walking through the aquarium you'll find jellyfish residing in the iconic smokestacks, exposed brick walls, coal tunnels, steel girders, and exhibits in the industrial pipes.

WHERE THE FISHES SWIM

WHAT Museum

WHERE 2000 Sycamore St.

COST $19.95

PRO TIP Don't miss walking through the shark tank, where four types of sharks live.

What do you do with an old streetcar powerhouse when streetcars go out of use? Turn part of it into an aquarium, of course, and make the smokestacks a main attraction where jellyfish live. © Deb Thompson

Around each corner is another surprise, and the aquarium has mastered using the old with the new to create a fun experience for visitors of all ages.

The Cleveland Aquarium melds an old building with a new aquarium to create a family-fun experience.

88

WORDEN'S LEDGES

Where can you find a sphinx in the Woods?

Worden's Ledges, located within the Hinckley Reservation, which is part of Cleveland Metroparks, is a hidden gem for nature lover's. The easy, one-mile path through a lush, green forest with large rock outcroppings covered in soft moss makes hikers forget about the outside world and marvel at the stone carvings and sculptures that appear along the path. The nine carvings range from a replica of the sphinx, to a four-foot-tall carving of Ty Cobb, to a rock carved to look like George Washington facing an oncoming army, to a bible and cross, to a simple word: "Nettie."

Nettie, refers to the wife of Noble Stuart, the son-in-law of Hiram Worden, a tombstone and statuary carver who owned the property until his death when it passed to his oldest daughter who inherited the estate. Upon her death, which some consider mysterious, the estate passed to Stuart who labored as a bricklayer and wannabe sculptor. Possibly to ease his guilt at the death of his beloved, or maybe to relieve his grief, he took to tinkering away and mastering his art on the sandstone ledges that presented a perfect canvas in the woods behind the property. The various pieces, fashioned between 1944 and 1948, have long outlived the artist himself.

Today you can see those carvings, etched into the rock walls in the forest, that have coexisted silently with nature for nearly seventy-five years.

WORDEN'S LEDGES

WHAT Public art

WHERE 895 Ledge Rd., Hinckley

COST Free

PRO TIP Pack a picnic lunch and spend time exploring the grounds and other trails within the park system.

A hike along the trail at Worden's Ledges leads to unexpected surprises among the large sandstone ledges on Hinckley Reservation.

89 WORLD'S LARGEST CANDY STORE

Do you have a sweet tooth?

This is the kind of place that would keep Willy Wonka on his toes! b.a. Sweetie Candy Co. is less of a traditional candy shop and more of a warehouse, with candy-laden industrial shelving that stretches floor to ceiling. Visitors will crane their necks as they decide whether to treat themselves to nostalgic candy, seasonal options, everyday family favorites, and more. A wall of Pez dispensers in every character imaginable brings out the kid in everyone, and a wall of jelly bean flavors means you only take home your favorites. Chocolates, suckers, gumballs, candy bars, boxed candy, gummies, and everything in between are stacked on shelves in bright colors—a feast for the eyes as much as it is for your sweet tooth.

This is the home of more than 4,500 different sweet items from 160 manufacturers, equaling about 500,000 pounds of candy. This larger-than-life candy store is a favorite for adults and children alike and is one of the few places you can still buy candy for a dime.

In addition to what feels like an endless array of candy, there is also an old-style soda shoppe that serves up unique floats and sundaes with their freshly made ice cream. With more than thirty-six flavors of ice cream made on site and more than two hundred soda pop varieties, there are thousands of options available and definitely something to tempt your taste buds. Candy store plus amazing soda shoppe makes this a one-of-a-kind find in Cleveland.

WORLD'S LARGEST CANDY STORE

WHAT b.a. Sweetie

WHERE 6770 Brookpark Rd.

COST Free

PRO TIP Take a selfie in front of the larger-than-life candy display.

The entrance to the World's Largest Candy Store is hard to miss with the massive, colorful swirled lollipop standing sentinel outside the entrance on a busy road near the interstate. © Deb Thompson

When there are over 4,500 sweet items to pick from, it's easy to give in to your sweet tooth at the World's Largest Candy Store.

90 WORLD'S LARGEST EAGLE'S NEST REPLICA

Has this nature center gone to the birds?

The Carlisle Visitor Center has gone to the birds. Literally. This Raptor Center, located near Lorain, is a haven for injured birds who undergo rehabilitation. These birds, including a bald eagle, screech owl, peregrine falcon, barred owl, and more, are unable to be released back in the wild, so they remain cared for in outdoor cages on the property, where they spread their wings for the rest of their days.

The center offers hiking trails, exhibits, and educational programming, but there is one aspect of the Raptor Center that couldn't be overlooked if you tried. A massive collection of sticks and twigs in the shape of a tornado form the World's Largest Eagle's Nest Replica. The nest is modeled after what is referred to as the "Great Nest," which could be seen in nearby Vermilion for a period of over thirty-five years, from 1890 until 1925, until a storm destroyed the tree it rested in.

Raptors aren't the only thing you'll see at the Raptor Center. Find out what the real show stopper is at this attraction.

THE WORLD'S LARGEST EAGLE'S NEST REPLICA

WHAT Roadside Attraction

WHERE 12882 Diagonal Rd., LaGrange

COST Free

PRO TIP Stop to see the eagle's nest, but don't leave without a walk on one of the trails.

The largest eagle's nest ever constructed weighed over 4,000 pounds. That's more than a Model T Ford! That Great Nest is long gone, but now you can see a replica of the original nest when you visit the Lorain Metroparks. © Tonya Prater

An typical eagle's nest can measure up to five feet wide and three feet deep, but the Great Nest, as it was called, measured in whopping 12 feet tall, 8½ feet wide, and weighed over 4,000 pounds! The Great Nest is the largest known nest ever constructed by a bird species. Today visitors to the center will find the replica, unveiled in March 2007, outside at the back of the Visitors Center.

INDEX